Welcome

Exciting jets, evocative warbirds, streamlined classic aeroplanes, tumbling aerobatics and smoke in the sky. National display teams with powerful fighters or brightly painted trainers. Twilight performances with fireworks and LED lights. Parachutists dropping from thousands of feet. Barnstorming recalling the flying circus era. Aircraft in blue skies against fluffy white clouds or in golden early-autumn light. Thunderous jet noise, rasping radial engines and scything rotor blades.

Airshows are all these sights and sounds and countless other moments – whether a poignant historical tribute, a jet bomber looming from a leaden sky, a huge airship flying past, the wind whistling over the wings of a glider or helicopters waltzing over coastal sands.

Beyond the aircraft, airshows are also about the anticipation of a day or weekend out. They are the excitement of arriving at the show, the first sight of massed tails or rows of aircraft in the morning light and taking in the landscape where the show will take place – whether the countryside beyond or the glistening sea.

Then there's the morning atmosphere at a show, wandering through a static park and browsing the displays, the scent of aviation fuel and freshly cut grass on the breeze, the sizzle of bacon or burgers on a grill, the hubbub of a crowd, music on the PA system, the click of cameras and smartphones pointed to the sky.

This special publication takes a comprehensive look at airshows as they are today. We look at spectacular display teams, fast jets, historic aeroplanes, helicopters and pyrotechnic air displays. We go behind the scenes to hear firsthand about displaying an F-16 fighter, piloting a Spitfire, being a wingwalker, leading an aerobatics team and even flying a biplane fitted with jet engines.

Join us for this in-depth look into an exciting world that each year gives millions of people countless memories for life.

Mark Broadbent
Editor

BELOW • *The Royal Australian Air Force Roulettes entertain the crowds at the Pacific Airshow on the Gold Coast, Australia.* CPL BRETT SHERRIFF/ROYAL AUSTRALIAN AIR FORCE

COVER PHOTO CREDITS
MAIN IMAGE • UK MOD/CROWN COPYRIGHT 2022 (UK EDITION), PETTY OFFICER 2ND CLASS EVAN DIAZ/US NAVY (REST OF WORLD EDITION)
INSET LEFT • 46 AVIATION CLASSICS
INSET CENTRE • NIGEL WATSON
INSET RIGHT • KAROLINA MAREK

CONTENTS

6 UK and Europe
Airshows and aviation events in 2025, from major international air displays to fly-ins

12 The Magic of Airshows
What's the big picture with airshows in the UK in 2025?

16 Red Arrows
The RAF Aerobatic Team prepares for another busy display season

20 Royal Air Force
From a frontline combat type to precision parachuting, the RAF on display

22 Navy Wings
A unique collection of naval air history, from wartime submarine-hunting to the Falklands

24 Army Flying
Helicopters and aircraft recall the history of UK army aviation

26 Starlings
High-performance displays from two champion aerobatic pilots

30 Spitfire
Flying and displaying a high-performance variant of the famous fighter

34 Flying the Flag
National display teams bring spectacle and style to airshows

42 Wingwalking
Display smoke, colour, noise and aerial acrobatics recall the flying circus era

48 North America
A huge variety of aircraft and shows across the continent

58 Worldwide
Airshows provide aerial entertainment and a platform for business all around the world

66 Fast Jets
The spectacle of modern and historic jets is a key element of airshows

68 Midlands Air Festival
From fast jets to the flying circus, hot air balloons and helicopters

70 Navy to Victory Tour
A rare historic aeroplane's 12,000-mile odyssey to mark 80 years since VE Day

72 Airship
A landmark anniversary for a widely recognised sight in the sky

74 Team Raven
Experienced pilots flying Van's RV-8 aircraft in an impressive formation aerobatic display team

78 Seaside
Coastal air displays are some of the most popular airshows

80 Pyro
Pyrotechnics, LEDs, smoke and light – dynamic displays bringing brightness to airshows

86 F-16
An F-16 is always a highlight at an airshow – especially in an eyecatching colour scheme

90 Gazelle Squadron
Colourful ex-military Gazelles provide a nostalgic presence at airshows

94 Flying Bulls
Red Bull sponsors numerous aircraft, from piston warbirds and jets to helicopters and aerobatics

98 Jet Pitts
Aerial entertainment from a classic aerobatic biplane fitted with jet turbines

104 Classics
There's a rich mix of historic aircraft flying in British skies each summer

110 RIAT
Organising the aircraft participation at the Royal International Air Tattoo at RAF Fairford

Contents

12

30

104

68

ISBN: 978 1 83632 090 6
Editor: Mark Broadbent
Senior editor, specials: Roger Mortimer
Email: roger.mortimer@keypublishing.com
Cover Design: Steve Donovan
Design: SJmagic DESIGN SERVICES, India
Advertising Sales Manager: Sam Clark
Email: sam.clark@keypublishing.com
Tel: 01780 755131
Advertising Production: Becky Antoniades
Email: Rebecca.antoniades@keypublishing.com

SUBSCRIPTION/MAIL ORDER
Key Publishing Ltd, PO Box 300, Stamford, Lincs, PE9 1NA
Tel: 01780 480404
Subscriptions email: subs@keypublishing.com
Mail Order email: orders@keypublishing.com
Website: www.keypublishing.com/shop

PUBLISHING
Group CEO and Publisher: Adrian Cox

Published by
Key Publishing Ltd, PO Box 100, Stamford, Lincs, PE9 1XQ
Tel: 01780 755131 **Website:** www.keypublishing.com

PRINTING
Precision Colour Printing Ltd, Haldane,
Halesfield 1, Telford, Shropshire. TF7 4QQ

DISTRIBUTION
Seymour Distribution Ltd, 2 Poultry Avenue, London, EC1A 9PU
Enquiries Line: 02074 294000.

We are unable to guarantee the bona fides of any of our advertisers. Readers are strongly recommended to take their own precautions before parting with any information or item of value, including, but not limited to money, manuscripts, photographs, or personal information in response to any advertisements within this publication.

© Key Publishing Ltd 2025
All rights reserved. No part of this magazine may be reproduced or transmitted in any form by any means, electronic or mechanical, including photocopying, recording or by any information storage and retrieval system, without prior permission in writing from the copyright owner. Multiple copying of the contents of the magazine without prior written approval is not permitted.

WWW.KEY.AERO AIRSHOWS OF THE WORLD 2025 5

UK AND EUROPE

UK and Europe

Airshows and aviation events in 2025, from major international air displays to fly-ins

LEFT • *The Paris Air Show at Le Bourget is this year's largest aerospace industry show.* ALEXANDRE DOUMENJOU/AIRBUS

United Kingdom

May 2025

02-04	**Sleap Airfield, Shropshire:**	Military Fly-In I www.shropshireaeroclub.com
03-04	**Popham Airfield, Hampshire:**	Microlight Trade Show I www.popham-airfield.co.uk
05	**London, UK:**	VE Day 80 Flypast
10	**IWM Duxford, Cambridgeshire:**	VE Day Flying Day I www.iwm.org.uk
11	**Old Warden Aerodrome, Bedfordshire:**	Shuttleworth Collection Season Premiere Airshow I www.shuttleworth.org
16-17	**Wycombe Air Park, Buckinghamshire:**	Private Flyer Fest South 2025 I www.privateflyershow.com/uk
17	**Bodmin Airfield, Cornwall:**	Ladies Day Fly-In I www.bodminairfield.com
17	**North Coates, Lincolnshire:**	Spring Flying Meeting I www.northcoatesflyingclub.com
17	**Popham Airfield, Hampshire:**	Vintage Piper Aircraft Club Meet I www.popham-airfield.co.uk
17-18	**Wickenby Airfield, Lincolnshire:**	Flour Bombing Competition I www.wickenbyairfield.com/2025-calender
24/26	**Lincolnshire Aviation Heritage Centre, East Kirkby, Lincolnshire:**	Lanc, Tank and Military Machines I www.lincsaviation.co.uk/events
25	**Stow Maries Aerodrome, Essex:**	Stow Maries Wings and Wheels I www.stowmaries.org
30-Jun 1	**Cotswold Airport, Kemble, Gloucestershire:**	Great Vintage Flying Weekend I www.cotswoldairport.com
30-Jun 1	**Ragley Hall, Warwickshire:**	Midlands Air Festival 2025 I www.midlandsairfestival.com
30-Jun 1	**Paignton seafront, Devon:**	English Riviera Airshow 2025 I www.englishrivieraairshow.co.uk
31	**Old Warden Aerodrome, Bedfordshire:**	Shuttleworth Collection Military Airshow I www.shuttleworth.org
31	**Compton Abbas Airfield, Wiltshire:**	Radial Day Fly-In I www.comptonairfield.com/events/radial-day-fly-in

June 2025

07	**IWM Duxford, Cambridgeshire:**	D-Day Flying Day I www.iwm.org.uk
07 or 08	**Breighton Airfield, East Yorkshire:**	Vintage Piper Cub Fly-In I www.realaero.com
08	**RAF Cosford, Shropshire:**	RAF Cosford Air Show 2025 I www.cosfordairshow.co.uk
08	**Stow Maries Aerodrome, Essex:**	Early Summer Fly-In I www.stowmaries.org
13-15	**Weston Park, Shropshire:**	Weston Park International Model Air Show 2025 I www.airshowinternational.co.uk
14	**The Mall, London:**	HM The King's Birthday Flypast

United Kingdom (contd.)

14	**Abingdon Airfield, Oxfordshire:** Abingdon Air & Country Show 2025	www.abingdonairandcountry.co.uk
14	**Blackbushe Airport, Surrey:** Blackbushe Air Day	www.blackbusheairday.com
14-15	**Breighton Airfield, East Yorkshire:** Annual Vintage Aircraft Club Fly-In	www.realaero.com
15	**Sleap Airfield, Shropshire:** Machine Meet – Summer 2025	www.shropshireaeroclub.com
21	**Bognor Regis seafront, West Sussex:** Bognor Regis Armed Forces Day
21	**Newtonards Airfield, Northern Ireland:** Northern Ireland Armed Forces Day 2025	www.visitardsandnorthdown.com/whats-on
21	**Shobdon Airfield, Herefordshire:** Shobdon Airfest '25	www.shobdonairfield.co.uk
21-22	**IWM Duxford, Cambridgeshire:** Duxford Summer Air Show	www.iwm.org.uk
22	**North Coates, Lincolnshire:** Whirlybird Sunday Helicopters & Gyros	www.northcoatesflyingclub.com
23-29	**Broad Chalke, Salisbury, Wiltshire:** Chalke History Festival	www.chalkefestival.com
27-29	**Cleethorpes seafront, Lincolnshire:** North East Lincolnshire Armed Forces Weekend	www.afmet.co.uk/armed-forces-day
27-28	**Leeds East Airport, Church Fenton, North Yorkshire:** Private Flyer Fest North 2025	www.privateflyershow.com/uk/leeds
28	**Compton Abbas Airfield, Wiltshire:** Stampe Saturday Fly-In	www.comptonairfield.com/events/stampe-saturday-fly-in
28	**Plymouth Hoe, Devon:** Plymouth Armed Forces Day 2025	www.plymoutharmedforcesday.co.uk
28	**Scarborough seafront, North Yorkshire:** Scarborough Armed Forces Day 2025	www.visitscarborough.com
28-29	**Breighton Airfield, East Yorkshire:** RV Club Fly-In	www.realaero.com
28-29	**Headcorn Aerodrome, Kent:** Battle of Britain Airshow	www.bobairshow.co.uk
28-29	**Heveningham Hall, Norfolk:** Heveningham Hall Country Fair and Concours	countryfair.co.uk
28-29	**Old Warden Aerodrome, Bedfordshire:** Shuttleworth Collection Festival of Flight	www.shuttleworth.org
29	**Ryde Esplanade, Isle of Wight, Hampshire:** Isle of Wight Armed Forces Day 2025	www.isleofwightarmedforcesday.co.uk

July 2025

05	**Blenheim Palace, Oxfordshire:** Battle Proms	www.battleproms.com
05-06	**Aldhurst Farm, Capel, Surrey:** Capel Military Show 2025	www.capelmilitaryshow.com
05-06	**Sleap Airfield, Shropshire:** Large Model Airshow	www.shropshireaeroclub.com
05-06	**Swansea Bay, South Wales:** Swansea Airshow 2025	www.walesnationalairshow.com
10-13	**Goodwood, West Sussex:** Goodwood Festival of Speed	ww.goodwood.com/motorsport/festival-of-speed
11-13	**Sleap Airfield, Shropshire:** SleapKosh 2025	www.shropshireaeroclub.com/sleapkosh
12	**Burghley House, Lincolnshire:** Battle Proms	www.battleproms.com
12	**Leeds Castle, Kent:** Leeds Castle Concert	www.leedscastleconcert
12	**Middle Wallop, Hampshire:** Wallop Wheels and Wings 2025	www.armyflying.com
12-13	**Breighton Airfield, East Yorkshire:** UK Vintage Aerobatic Competition	www.realaero.com
12-13	**North Coates Airfield, Lincolnshire:** Wings & Wheels	www.northcoatesflyingclub.com
18-20	**RAF Fairford, Gloucestershire:** Royal International Air Tattoo 2025	www.airtattoo.com
19	**Hatfield Park, Hertfordshire:** Battle Proms	www.battleproms.com
25	**IWM Duxford, Cambridgeshire:** The Americans Flying Day	www.iwm.org.uk
26	**Old Warden Aerodrome, Bedfordshire:** Shuttleworth Collection Summer Air Show	www.shuttleworth.org
26-27	**Old Buckenham Airfield, Norfolk:** Old Buckenham Airshow 2025	www.oldbuckenhamairshow.com
31-Aug 01	**Old Warden Aerodrome, Bedfordshire:** DH.600 – The Centenary of the de Havilland Moth	www.dhmothclub.co.uk

August 2025

02	**Highclere Castle, Hampshire:** Battle Proms	www.battleproms.com
02	**Lincolnshire Aviation Heritage Centre, East Kirkby, Lincolnshire:** East Kirkby Airshow 2025	www.lincsaviation.co.uk/events
02-03	**Withernsea, Nouth Yorkshire:** Blue Light Weekend	www.bluelightweekend.com
08-10	**Ashton Court, Bristol:** Bristol International Balloon Fiesta 2025	www.bristolballoonfiesta.co.uk
09-10	**Blackpool seafront, Lancashire:** Blackpool Airshow 2025	www.visitblackpool.com
13	**Falmouth, Cornwall:** Falmouth Week 2025	www.falmouthweek.co.uk
14-17	**Eastbourne seafront, West Sussex:** Eastbourne International Airshow 2025	www.visiteastbourne.com/airshow
15-17	**Sleap Airfield, Shropshire:** 1940s Weekender	www.1940sweekender.com
16	**Breighton Airfield, East Yorkshire:** G for George Day	www.realaero.com
16	**Compton Abbas Airfield, Wiltshire:** De Havilland Day Fly-In	www.comptonairfield.com/events/de-havilland-day-fly-in
16	**IWM Duxford, Cambridgeshire:** Flying Evening	www.iwm.org.uk
16	**Old Warden Aerodrome, Bedfordshire:** Shuttleworth Collection Flying Proms	www.shuttleworth.org
16-17	**Manston Airport, Kent:** Manston International Airshow	www.manstoninternationalairshow.com
20	**Cromer seafront, Norfolk:** Cromer Carnival Air Displays	www.cromercarnival.co.uk
21-22	**Clacton-on-Sea seafront, Essex:** Clacton Airshow 2025	www.clactonairshow.com
22	**Sidmouth seafront, East Devon:** Sidmouth Regatta Airshow	www.visitdevon.co.uk/sidmouth/whats-on
23	**Compton Abbas Airfield, Wiltshire:** Summer Vintage Fly-In	www.comptonairfield.com/events/summer-vintage-fly-in-weekend
24	**Little Gransden Airfield, Cambridgeshire:** Little Gransden Air and Car Show	www.littlegransdenairshow.co.uk
24	**Stow Maries Aerodrome, Essex:** Stow Maries Air Show	www.stowmaries.org

UK AND EUROPE

United Kingdom (contd.)

25-26	**Henstridge Airfield, Somerset:**	Henstridge Wings & Wheels	www.wingsandwheelshenstridge.com
29-31	**Foxlands Farm, Cosby, Leicestershire:**	Victory Show 2025	www.thevictoryshow.co.uk
29-31	**Leicester Airport, Leicestershire:**	LAA Rally 2025	www.lightaircraftassociation.co.uk/laa-rally-2025
30	**Old Warden Aerodrome, Bedfordshire:**	Shuttleworth Collection Best of British Airshow	www.shuttleworth.org
30-31	**Southport seafront, Merseyside:**	Southport Airshow	www.visitsouthport.com

September 2025

05-06	**Ayr seafront, South Ayrshire, Scotland:**	The International Ayr Show – Festival of Flight	www.destinationsouthayrshire.co.uk/ayrshow
06	**Bodmin Airfield, Cornwall:**	Cornwall Strut Fly-In	www.bodminairfield.com
06-07	**IWM Duxford, Cambridgeshire:**	Battle of Britain Air Show	www.iwm.org.uk
06-07	**North Coates, Lincolnshire:**	Summer Fly-In	www.northcoatesflyingclub.com
10	**St Peter Port, Guernsey:**	Guernsey Battle of Britain Air Display	www.guernseyairdisplay.com
11	**St Helier, Jersey:**	Jersey International Air Display	www.jerseyairdisplay.org.uk
12-14	**Longleat, Wiltshire:**	Longleat Icons of the Sky	www.longleat.co.uk/icons-of-the-sky
12-14	**Goodwood Aerodrome, West Sussex:**	Goodwood Revival 2025	www.goodwood.com/motorsport/goodwood-revival
19-20	**Sleap Airfield, Shropshire:**	Sleap Air-Day 2025	www.shropshireaeroclub.com
19-21	**Lee-on-Solent Airfield, Hampshire:**	Lee Victory Festival	www.leevictoryfestival.co.uk
20-21	**Sywell Aerodrome, Northamptonshire:**	Sywell Classic – Pistons and Props	www.sywellclassic.co.uk
27	**Compton Abbas Airfield, Wiltshire:**	Microlight Fly-In	www.comptonairfield.com/events/microlight-fly-in
30-Oct 01	**London ExCel Exhibition Centre, London:**	Helitech Expo	www.helitech.co.uk

October 2025

04	**Compton Abbas Airfield, Wiltshire:**	Autumn Vintage Fly-In	www.comptonairfield.com/events/autumn-vintage-fly-in
04	**IWM Duxford, Cambridgeshire:**	Flying Finale	www.iwm.org.uk
05	**Old Warden Aerodrome, Bedfordshire:**	Shuttleworth Collection Race Day	www.shuttleworth.org
17	**Sleap Airfield, Shropshire:**	Machine Meet – Autumn 2025	www.shropshireaeroclub.com

All details correct as of April 2025 and subject to change. This listing does not include events closed to the public, including private military events/family days.

FAR LEFT • *Spitfire XIV MV293/G-SPIT in its Indian Air Force livery.* JAMIE EWAN

LEFT • *Saab B 17A SE-BYH, pictured here at Duxford in 2024, is operated by the Swedish Air Force Historic Flight.* NIGEL WATSON

LEFT • *Patrouille Suisse are scheduled for displays in Switzerland, Spain (AIRE25 in June) and Italy (Rivolto in September).* LIONEL BONAVENTURE/AFP VIA GETTY IMAGES

RIGHT • *North American T-6s at La Ferté Alais, France.* PAUL JOHNSON

Europe

May 2025

07	**Beauchevain, Belgium:**	Beauchevain Air Base Day | www.babday.be
10	**Muret-Lherm, France:**	AirExpo | www.airexpo.org
11	**Rimini, Italy:**	Frecce Tricolori display
16-18	**Friedrichshafen, Germany:**	Klassikwelt Bodensee | www.klassikwelt-bodensee.de
17-18	**Le Touquet seafront, France:**	Le Touquet Air Show | https://www.letouquet.com/agenda/meeting-aerien-le-touquet-air-show
18	**Desenzano Del Garda, Italy:**	Frecce Tricolori display
18	**Sabadell Airport, Spain:**	Fundació Parc Aeronàutic de Catalunya Open Day | www.fpac.org/calendar
25	**Grado, Italy:**	Frecce Tricolori display
30-31	**Altenrhein, Switzerland:**	Airshow Hoher Kasten | www.hoherkasten.ch/airshow
30-Jun 1	**Biscarrosse, France:**	Reassemblement International d'Hydroavions 2025 | www.hydravions-biscarrosse.com/rassemblement-international-d-hydravions.php
31-Jun 01	**BAN Hyères, Toulon, France:**	Portes Ouvertes - 100 ans de la BAN d'Hyères | www.hyeres2025.fr

June 2025

01	**Kjeller Airfield, Lillestrøm, Norway:**	Kjeller Flydag 2025 | www.flydagen.com
05	**Ladispoli, Italy:**	Frecce Tricolori display
05-07	**Lyon-Bron Airport, France:**	France Air Expo 2025 | www.franceairexpo.com
07-08	**Cerny-La Ferté-Alais, France:**	Fete Aerienne Les Temps des Hélices | www.letempsdeshelices.fr
07-08	**Pardubice Airfield, Czech Republic:**	Aviatická Pouť – Pardubice Aviation Fair | www.aviatickapout.cz
07-08	**Tartu, Estonia:**	Estonian Aviation Days | www.lennundusmuuseum.ee/en
08	**Punta Marina, Italy:**	Frecce Tricolori display
13-15	**Gelnhausen, Germany:**	Flugplatz-Kerb | www.flugplatzkerb-gelnhausen.de
14-15	**Kauhava Airport, Finland:**	Kauhava Airshow 2025 | www.kauhavaairshow.com
14-15	**San Javier, Spain:**	AIRE2025 | www.aire25.es
14-15	**Spilve Airport, Riga, Latvia:**	Baltic International Airshow | www.balticairshow.com
15	**Playa Granada, Motril, Granada, Spain:**	Festival Aéreo de Motril | www.motrilairshow.com
14-15	**Dolné Považie, Slovakia:**	Festival letectva Piešťany | www.festivalletectva.sk
15	**Sabadell Airport, Spain:**	Fundació Parc Aeronàutic de Catalunya Open Day | www.fpac.org/calendar
16-22	**Le Bourget Airport, Paris, France:**	Paris Air Show – Salon International de l'Aéronautique et de l'Espace du Bourget | www.siae.fr
19-22	**Flugplatz Kehl-Sundheim, Kehl, Germany:**	Kehler Flugtage | www.kehler-flugtage.de
20-21	**Leszno, Poland:**	Antidotum Airshow Leszno 2025 | www.antidotumairshow.pl
22	**Giorgio, Italy:**	Frecce Tricolori display
27-28	**Tábor airfield, Tábor, Czechia:**	Slet československých letadel | www.scsl.cz
28	**Fliegerhorst Bückeberg, Germany:**	Tag der Bundeswehr | www.bundeswehr.de

WWW.KEY.AERO **AIRSHOWS OF THE WORLD 2025** 9

BIG PICTURE

The Magic of Airshows

What's the big picture with airshows in the UK in 2025?

Airshows in the UK are in a good spot, says British Air Displays Association (BADA) chairman Matt Wilkins: "The message from airshows is very simple, and it contrasts with what we hear from the rest of the events industry. The two words we as organisers have among us consistently are 'sold' and 'out'."

BADA's Air Display Industry Review 2024 said the estimated total crowd figure for UK airshows in 2024 was 4.2 million people. It continued: "It is likely that the [UK] air display industry holds the position as the fourth most popular outdoor event sector after football, horse racing and music festivals."

Matt explained: "For many years, airshows said 'We're the third-biggest spectator industry [in the UK] after football and horseracing'. Turns out the music festival business wasn't promulgating their crowd numbers. Now they are, and it transpires we've always been number four, but we are *firmly* number four."

New events

BADA noted in its report that "2024 was generally a successful season for the air display industry."

Indeed, the association said, attendances were probably suppressed. Three seaside air displays with large crowds usually held at the August/September summer season peak (Folkestone, Sidmouth, Rhyl) cancelled in 2024 because the Red Arrows were unavailable owing to the team's tour of Canada. Three other large seaside shows that did take place (Bournemouth, Ayr, Portrush) also missed the Red Arrows, and the team only displayed on the first of Eastbourne's four days.

Still, BADA's report noted record crowds elsewhere. There were also new shows, including the Golden Age of Aviation Airshow at Compton Abbas Airfield in Dorset, run by Aero Legends, the organiser of the Battle of Britain Airshow at Headcorn in Kent.

Lee on Solent Airfield in Hampshire (the former HMS Daedalus) marked the 80th anniversary of D-Day. Longleat in Wiltshire held the Sky Safari, which expanded the estate's annual hot air balloon gathering into a four-day event comprising a two-hour air show, pyrotechnic displays, balloon launches/nightglows and fireworks.

Another new event, the Sywell Airshow in Northamptonshire, was praised for including overseas aircraft never seen in the UK before, such as the Boeing Stearman wingwalking act from 46 Aviation in Switzerland

BELOW • *Aero Legends' C-47A Skytrain N473DC Drag 'em oot at the Headcorn Battle of Britain Airshow in Kent in 2024.*
PAUL JOHNSON

ABOVE • *Airshows are one of the most popular spectator activities in the UK. British seaside airshows, like Blackpool, attracted a combined total of 2.8 million spectators in 2024.*
VISITBLACKPOOL

and a warbird quartet from Red Bull Flying Bulls in Austria comprising a Chance Vought Corsair, Lockheed P-38 Lightning, North American P-51 Mustang and North American B-25 Mitchell.

Overshadowing the positivity, 2024 saw the loss of several individuals involved in UK airshows. Strikemaster Display Team founder Mark Petrie passed away just before the season began. RAF Battle of Britain Memorial Flight fighter pilot, Squadron Leader Mark Long, was lost in a Spitfire accident at RAF Coningsby in Lincolnshire in May. Later in the year came the sad news about the passing of Richard Grace, the experienced display pilot and a major figure in the UK's warbird community, who led the small team that put together the Sywell Airshow.

A December 2024 Sywell show statement said: "Sadly, just a short time ago, Richard lost his battle with illness, which has left a huge hole in the airshow community. Richard was the driving force for Sywell 2024 and it was his idea to do a show that contained the elements that he'd like to see at the perfect airshow.

"The team has decided that we sign off on a high note, and thus Sywell 2024 will remain a one-off show. We are sure that Sywell Aerodrome will one day host another airshow, but the team behind the 2024 show are leaving the great memories with you, as Richard's vision, a testament and legacy to a great man."

Huge crowds

BADA chairman Matt Wilkins is the event organiser of the Old Buckenham Airshow and is the aerodrome manager of the Norfolk airfield. Matt said that UK airshow audience numbers were "in marked contrast to what the rest of the events industry seem to be reporting. They speak of costs going up, audiences falling and doom and gloom. There are a few exceptions – places like Goodwood sell out all day, every day, because they are the very best at what they do and offer – but in the wider events industry, there's a malaise.

"Talking with contractors for my airshow, one said that business otherwise is so bad they fear they'd be bust without our event. This is a large and well-established events industry contractor; if you have people like that saying they're having a bad time with bookings and business, that tells you there's a problem."

Airshows are bucking this trend, Matt emphasised: "The airshow industry, it seems, is beating just about every other event there is. The magic of airshows has not diminished. Plenty of people say the demise of the airshow is inevitable, but there's absolutely no evidence of that whatsoever. In fact, all evidence points completely the other way."

The Royal International Air Tattoo at RAF Fairford in Gloucestershire – the UK's largest airshow if measured by the number of aircraft present – reported 168,000 visitors in 2024. At the time of writing in January 2025 – at which point not a single aircraft participant had been announced – RIAT reported 50,000 tickets had already been sold and three premium enclosures for the Saturday had sold out for the forthcoming July 2025 show. BADA's report noted that in 2024, RIAT completely sold out of both general admission tickets and hospitality upgrade options, and that all three public show days sold out in advance of the show weekend for the first time.

Many other shows saw large crowds in 2024, reported BADA. The Royal Air Force Cosford Air Show in Shropshire – the last RAF-organised air display – drew a crowd of 60,000. The Imperial War Museum Duxford, Cambridgeshire and the Shuttleworth Collection at Old Warden, Bedfordshire reported increased footfall compared with earlier years.

Established events are not the only venues doing well. "There are new airshows, and they're selling out," Matt said. "Traditionally, [organisers] always lose money on their first one, but that did not happen."

Seaside airshows, which are mostly free to attend, have the largest crowd numbers of any UK air events. According to BADA's review, the 15 seafront shows around the British Isles in 2024 (Jersey and Guernsey are Crown Dependencies and not

RED ARROWS

Islands. Describing how Red Arrows flying compares to his previous posting, he said: "The skillset of close formation flying is used regularly on the frontline and is a vital tool to be able to employ in various situations. However, the Red Arrows take this to the next level. The precision, teamwork and trust required to fly in large, dynamic formations close to the ground is a totally new skill, almost like learning to fly again."

For Red 3, flying the Red Arrows' BAE Systems Hawk TMk1 aircraft represents a major change from Flt Lt McEwen's previous role piloting the Lockheed Martin F-35B Lightning II, the RAF's fifth-generation multi-role aircraft. The Wexham, Berkshire born pilot said: "The F-35B has the wonder of modern technology, autopilot and superior situational awareness. The Hawk T1 has none of that, and, in many ways, is a true pilot's machine that involves raw flying – not to mention, when part of the Red Arrows, flown as part of one of the largest aerobatic formations in the world. This requires a new type of focus, concentration, and trust.

"I first saw the Red Arrows flying on the wing of a Concorde above my house when I was about five years old. I remember it vividly. From that moment the goal of becoming a Red Arrow, and thus RAF pilot, was born, and it influenced my entire adolescent journey. The pinnacle of professionalism and perfection in the air really appealed to me, as well as the shear fun it looked. I wanted to join the Red Arrows so I could inspire future generations to join the RAF, just as I was – a chance to give back."

Flt Lt McEwen flew the F-35B Lightning on 617 Squadron, the 'Dambusters', based at RAF Marham in Norfolk. He said: "It was the happiest moment in my career when I learned I'd got the job [on the Red Arrows]. The news was given to me by my boss at the time, Officer Commanding 617 Sqn, Wing Commander Stew Campbell.

"Having invited me to his office, it was a delightful shock to discover why. As a personal mentor and an ex-Red Arrows pilot himself, it was a wonderful moment. I then phoned my father immediately, whose words were 'No way!' I think he was more shocked than me!".

2025 display

The Red Arrows have three versions of their display – full, rolling, flat – that are interchangeable, enabling the team to optimise for weather conditions and any airspace restrictions.

Winter/spring training sorties at RAF Waddington showed what's in store for

Red Arrows Displays 2025

Date	Event	Location
May		
05	VE Day 80 Flypast	The Mall, London, UK
24	Chania	Crete, Greece
26	Thessaloniki	Thessaloniki, Greece
30	Midlands Air Festival	Ragley Hall, Worcestershire
31	Midlands Air Festival	Ragley Hall, Worcestershire
31	English Riviera Airshow	Paignton, Devon
June		
01	English Riviera Airshow	Paignton, Devon
01	Midlands Air Festival	Ragley Hall, Worcestershire
05	Isle of Man TT Races	Douglas, Isle of Man
08	RAF Cosford Air Show	RAF Cosford, Shropshire
14	HM The King's Birthday Flypast	The Mall, London
15	AIRE2025	San Javier, Spain
21	Northern Ireland Armed Forces Day 2025	Newtonards Airfield, Northern Ireland
22	Duxford Summer Air Show 2025	IWM Duxford, Cambridgeshire
28	Armed Forces Day North East Lincolnshire	Cleethorpes, Lincolnshire
28	Shuttleworth Collection Festival of Flight	Old Warden, Bedfordshire
29	Battle of Britain Airshow	Headcorn, Kent
29	Event details TBC	Event details TBC
July		
05	Wales Airshow	Swansea Bay, Wales
06	Formula One British Grand Prix Flypast	Silverstone, Northamptonshire
06	Wales Airshow	Swansea Bay, Wales
10	Goodwood Festival of Speed	Goodwood, West Sussex
11	Goodwood Festival of Speed	Goodwood, West Sussex
13	Goodwood Festival of Speed	Goodwood, West Sussex
18	Royal International Air Tattoo	RAF Fairford, Gloucestershire
19	Royal International Air Tattoo	RAF Fairford, Gloucestershire
20	Royal International Air Tattoo	RAF Fairford, Gloucestershire
21	The Tall Ships Races	Aberdeen, Scotland
26	Swanage Carnival	Swanage, Dorset
26	Old Buckenham Airshow	Old Buckenham, Norfolk
27	Old Buckenham Airshow	Old Buckenham, Norfolk
August		
09	Blackpool Airshow	Blackpool, Lancashire
09	Royal Edinburgh Military Tattoo Flypast	Edinburgh, Scotland
10	Blackpool Airshow	Blackpool, Lancashire
13	Falmouth Week	Falmouth, Cornwall
14	Eastbourne International Airshow	Eastbourne, West Sussex
15	Eastbourne International Airshow	Eastbourne, West Sussex
16	Eastbourne International Airshow	Eastbourne, West Sussex
17	Eastbourne International Airshow	Eastbourne, West Sussex
20	Cromer Carnival	Cromer, Norfolk
21	Clacton Airshow	Clacton-on-Sea, Essex
22	Clacton Airshow	Clacton-on-Sea, Essex
22	Sidmouth Regatta	Sidmouth, Devon
24	Roskilde Airshow	Roskilde, Denmark
30	Bucharest International Airshow – flypast	Bucharest, Romania
30	Radom Airshow	Radom, Poland
31	Radom Airshow	Radom, Poland
September		
05	International Ayr Show – Festival of Flight	Ayr, Scotland
06	International Ayr Show – Festival of Flight	Ayr, Scotland
07	Great North Run	South Shields, Tyne & Wear
10	Guernsey Air Display	St Peter Port, Guernsey, Channel Islands
11	Jersey International Air Display	St Aubin's Bay, St Helier, Jersey, Channel Islands
13	Sanicole Airshow	Sanicole, Belgium
14	Sanicole Airshow	Sanicole, Belgium
20	NATO Days	Ostrava, Czechia
21	NATO Days	Ostrava, Czechia
27	Overseas event, details TBC	Overseas event, details TBC
28	Overseas event, details TBC	Overseas event, details TBC
October		
04	Duxford Flying Finale	IWM Duxford, Cambridgeshire

TBC denotes to be confirmed at the time of writing. This listing is subject to change and does not include private military events.

2025. Big Battle, the large V-shaped formation, returns as the opening manoeuvre. Diamond Nine, Nine Arrow, Concorde, Apollo and Big Vixen are other shapes in this year's first half.

Two formations, Swan and Typhoon, both return after a few seasons away. In Red Arrows terminology, these shapes are 'long' and 'wide'. Aircraft are positioned several lengths behind Red 1, the pilots' reference point, and the two outermost aircraft are widely separated. Typhoon formation, representing the RAF's multirole combat aircraft, is in the show exactly 50 years since the team first flew the shape. Back then, it was called Viggen.

Each year's Red Arrows display sees pilot/crowd favourite manoeuvres blended with new or revived figures, with subtle tweaks to how everything links together, so the routine slightly changes year to year when you look closely.

New in the second half in 2025 is a manoeuvre called Chainsaw, involving all four aircraft of Hanna section. Another manoeuvre, Twister, sees Red 5 flying tight barrel rolls around the other four aircraft in Enid.

There's an entirely new finale for the full height display sequence for 2025. The Palm Split, where seven aircraft (Enid, and Reds 8/9) pull up into a fan split to inscribe the shape of a palm tree in the sky, is co-ordinated with opposition barrel rolls from the Synchro Pair.

Mainstays in the display include the Hanna Break, Hanna Pass, Heart, Vertical Break, Rollbacks and the various Synchro opposition passes. The Serpent returns, where Enid fly an arcing barrel roll before heading into a tight 360° turn and changing into a line-abreast shape called Tango. The 5/4 Cross sees all nine aircraft crossing over – the five aircraft of Enid from the left-hand side of the display line, and the four jets of Hanna from the right.

'Timeless'

Any event organiser can apply for a Red Arrows display. The RAF Events Team collates the bids and decides where the team performs. A display allocation is significant for event organisers.

Zbyněk Pavlačík is the chairman of Jagello 2000, which runs the NATO Days airshow at Ostrava in Czechia. Pavlačík said: "The Red Arrows' first participation [in 2006] significantly contributed to the international prestige of our event and opened the doors to Ostrava for other exclusive foreign participants. They presented themselves here for the second time in 2012, and NATO Days have transformed beyond recognition."

This year is NATO Days' 25th anniversary, and the Red Arrows will perform two displays. "We are so honoured that we can announce such a significant group as the first participant in this anniversary year, and we are happy that they are returning to us after so many years," Pavlačík said.

A Red Arrows display means a great deal too for events that are not principally airshows, such as carnivals or regattas, but which receive a display allocation. Swanage Carnival in Dorset will have a display in 2025 for the first time in eight years. Carnival chairman Kevin Langdon told *Swanage News*: "This is a fantastic attraction for our carnival and a major boost for the town. The Red Arrows are world renowned for their precision and skill and having them as part of our event is a true honour."

Further along the south coast is Torbay in Devon, where the English Riviera Airshow will host two Red Arrows displays in 2025. The event's organisers highlight the team's "timeless spectacle" and this, perhaps, explains their enduring appeal through the decades.

From the 1960s to the age of smartphones, the Red Arrows have been part of the fabric of Britain. It just seems fitting for the red jets to be part of national life, for their colourful signature to be in the sky. ●

ABOVE • *Reds 6-9 form Hanna section, named after the legendary Red 1 of the late 1960s, Ray Hanna.* MIDLANDS AIR FESTIVAL

BELOW • *A unique angle on the Goose in a photo entitled 'Smoke and Splendour'.* UK MINISTRY OF DEFENCE/CROWN COPYRIGHT 2024

Royal Air Force

From frontline combat to precision parachuting, the RAF on display

ABOVE • The BBMF Lancaster (PA474), built in Chester, will be 80 years old in 2025. NIGEL WATSON

The Royal Air Force Eurofighter Typhoon FGR4 solo display is always impressive, bringing a thunderous presence to proceedings wherever it appears.

Seven frontline RAF units comprising 1(F), II(AC), 3(F), 6, IX(B), 12 and XI(F) Squadrons operate the multirole Typhoon. It is a busy force, undertaking quick reaction alert air defence for UK and Falkland Islands airspace, and missions supporting NATO air defence in the Baltic and Black Sea regions. Typhoons also deploy on Operation Shader, the RAF's ongoing commitment to combating IS in Iraq and Eastern Syria.

The Typhoon display is provided by 29 Squadron, the Typhoon Operational Conversion Unit, at RAF Coningsby in Lincolnshire. Squadron Leader Nathan Shawyer, call-sign 'REHEAT01', is the display pilot in 2025.

Work-up

It has been two decades since the RAF introduced the Typhoon display in 2005. In that time, several RAF fast jets that were once UK airshow stalwarts – the Harrier, Tornado, Jaguar and Hawk – have all retired from service, meaning Typhoon is the last remaining RAF solo fast jet display. (There was a role demonstration with the fifth-generation Lockheed Martin F-35B Lightning from RAF Marham at several 2024 airshows, but the Lightning Force's continued build-up means aircraft, crews and flying hours are unavailable for a display this year.)

Each year's RAF Typhoon display pilot designs their routine. There is no set sequence they must follow, so the routine slightly changes season by season (although it always contains previously approved manoeuvres). The pilot must design a full display – a 'high' show in other air forces' parlance – and limited and 'flat' versions for poor weather conditions. The Typhoon simulators at Coningsby are used to prepare these sequences before flying them for real. The display work-up starts with practices at 5,000ft, before progressively 'stepping down' in base heights. There is a predefined number of practices at each height. The final display height for Typhoon is 500ft for aerobatic manoeuvres, with level turns and flypasts conducted at 300ft and 100ft respectively. Training culminates with the award of Public Display Authority by Air Officer Commanding 1 Group.

Display

The RAF Typhoon display routine typically includes plenty of maximum-performance turns with afterburner, barrel rolls where the aircraft corkscrews and appears to 'skid' through the sky, and classic aerobatic manoeuvres including fast aileron rolls, hesitation rolls and vertical figures such as a loop, half-Cuban eights and half-horizontal eights.

Spring practices at Coningsby showed that Sqn Ldr Shawyer's sequence for 2025 includes all of these familiar elements. There's also an outside turn showing the top surfaces of the wings – an especially uncomfortable manoeuvre for the pilot, who has to pull negative G, but ideal for photographers.

Another eyecatching manoeuvre sees the Typhoon approach the crowd at a 45° angle, before pitching up for a barrel roll. The aircraft decelerates rapidly, giving the optical illusion it is suspended in flight.

The fly-by-wire flight control system manages the Typhoon's energy, enabling the aircraft to fly slowly without entering a stall. Reheat on the Eurojet EJ200 engines is engaged and the Typhoon powers into a loop.

Support team

Airshow audiences see a single pilot flying a single Typhoon, but an extensive team works behind the scenes to make the display happen.

The RAF Typhoon Display Team is an appropriate name. A management team plans the display season, co-ordinating everything from engineering resources and logistics support to managing sponsorship agreements, liaising with event organisers and flying display directors and securing diplomatic clearances for overseas displays.

Engineers and technicians from 29 Squadron work on the display Typhoon (and a second jet sent as a spare) at display venues/operating bases. The engineers are split into three teams named Lightning, Phantom and Tornado, all former 29 Squadron types. Led by a highly experienced and qualified RAF engineer, each team consists of five technicians from mechanical engineering, avionics and weapons systems backgrounds. This mix of specialist trade skills ensures any technical issues are swiftly rectified. All Typhoon Display Team members are volunteers and their contribution is in addition to their normal squadron duties and working hours.

Typically, the Typhoon team performs around 30 individual displays through the summer season at venues ranging from the Royal International Air Tattoo at RAF Fairford to humble grass airfields, seaside airshows and overseas bases.

BBMF

The Battle of Britain Memorial Flight (BBMF) at RAF Coningsby endured a tragic year in 2024. One of the flight's fighter pilots, Squadron Leader Mark Long, was killed in May when Supermarine Spitfire LF MkIXe MK356 crashed outside Coningsby.

The BBMF is airshow royalty in the UK, an indelible part of the aviation summer. Typically, its Spitfires, Hawker Hurricanes, Avro Lancasters (PA474) and Douglas C-47 Dakotas (ZA947) make hundreds of appearances nationwide each summer, from displays at large airshows to flypasts at all manner of fêtes, carnivals and local events.

In 2024, however, as investigations continued into the Coningsby accident, only the Lancaster was permitted to return to flight, while the fighters all remained grounded. The bomber was the BBMF's sole presence at airshows that year as the Dakota was unavailable due to its latest 'major' maintenance overhaul.

In March 2025, the BBMF provided an update about its plans for the forthcoming season: "BBMF are pleased to announce we will be flying our Merlin engine fighters this display season. Alongside our Lancaster, and after the return of our Dakota from the extended planned maintenance, all aircraft types will be flying again this year. We look forward to seeing you around the country and having a great display season celebrating the 85th anniversary of the Battle of Britain and 80th anniversaries of VE and VJ Day."

Squadron Leader Paul Wise, one of the Flight's bomber pilots, will be the next BBMF Officer Commanding in October 2025 for the 2026/27 display seasons, BBMF announced in January 2025.

The Falcons

Based at RAF Brize Norton in Oxfordshire, the RAF Falcons is the UK's only centrally funded, professional military parachute display team.

The RAF is responsible for training and supporting all UK military parachuting. Falcons team members are instructors with the Airborne Delivery Wing at Brize Norton, who undertake continual advanced training for future employment on duties supporting the Parachute Regiment, the Royal Marines and other specialist units.

The Falcons' website says: "Display parachuting is one of the most difficult types of parachuting and requires hard work, a high level of skill and, most importantly, trust in other team members and their equipment."

Established in 1965, the team's spectacular displays involve team members free-falling at speeds of up to 120mph after leaving the team's Dornier 228 aircraft. The Falcons perform various movements across the sky in freefall using coloured smoke to draw an aerial pattern. Team members then fly under canopy for manoeuvres called the Heart, Criss-Cross Carousel, Snakes and Ducks and The Sabre Chase, before completing controlled and accurate landings, sometimes into confined areas near buildings or water.

The website explains: "The aims of the Falcons have changed enormously over the decades. In addition to completing displays, there is a requirement for team members to qualify as Military Free Fall Instructors and High Altitude Instructors by the end of their three-year tour. During their time with the Falcons, each team member will accumulate 1,000 jumps, many of which are on training detachments worldwide."

The Falcons have performed in front of millions of people over the years, as far afield as Australia. As well as airshows, they frequently appear at agricultural shows or sporting events. "It is a great honour to be an RAF Falcon, demonstrating skills and promoting the RAF to the general public," the team's website says.

Tutor

The Grob Tutor TMk1 is the RAF's elementary flying trainer used by RAF University Air Squadrons and Air Experience Flights. The 2025 airshow season marks 25 years since the RAF introduced the Tutor display, which these days is provided by 115 Squadron at RAF Wittering in Cambridgeshire. Flight Lieutenant Bob Dewes is the display pilot.

According to the official website: "For display flying, the Tutor is not as powerful as purpose-built aerobatic display aircraft, but this makes for an interesting and challenging display as energy – a combination of speed and height – must be maintained between manoeuvres." This is "only possible through smooth and precise handling by the pilot. It may not be the largest, loudest or fastest aircraft on the circuit, but this gives the pilot opportunity to show their skill and finesse."

Chinook

A Chinook from RAF Odiham has previously been an RAF airshow asset, but there was no dedicated display for the 2024 season due to ongoing global operational commitments. Instead, a role demo showcased the aircraft's ability to support ground forces with underslung loads at several events.

Although operated by the RAF, the Chinook Force is managed by Joint Aviation Command (formerly Joint Helicopter Command). At the time of writing in March 2025, there has been no announcement about whether there would be a Chinook display/demo in 2025. ●

RIGHT • *The RAF Typhoon display is from 29 Squadron at RAF Coningsby.* UK MINISTRY OF DEFENCE/CROWN COPYRIGHT

BELOW • *The RAF Falcons represents the forces around the world. Here, it's at Gold Coast in Australia in 2024.* AUSTRALIAN DEPARTMENT OF DEFENCE

NAVY WINGS

Navy Wings

A unique collection celebrating naval air history, from wartime submarine-hunting to the Falklands

Navy Wings at Royal Naval Air Station Yeovilton in Somerset restores, maintains and flies historic fixed and rotary wing aircraft to tell the tale of British naval aviation.

It says: "The development of Britain's great naval aviation heritage is one of the most remarkable stories of the past 100 years. It's a story of epic achievement, heroic and daring actions and world-leading technological advancement that radically shaped history."

The Fly Navy Heritage Trust aims to educate the public in the history, traditions and exploits of the Fleet Air Arm, providing a living memorial to the men and women who served and inspiring future generations.

Background

Navy Wings' lineage goes back to the Royal Navy Historic Flight (RNHF), established at Yeovilton in 1972 to keep the Royal Navy's aviation heritage in the public eye. Over the years, the RNHF has displayed various types, including the Swordfish, Sea Hawk, Sea Fury and Firefly. It was stood down on March 31, 2019, after it became unsustainable for the UK Ministry of Defence (MOD) to continue to directly fund the RNHF. Without alternative funding, its aircraft faced an uncertain future.

Happily, the Royal Navy gifted the RNHF fleet to Navy Wings, securing its long-term future flying as civilian rather than military aircraft. Navy Wings and the Fly Navy Heritage Trust had supported RNHF activities since the mid-1990s with annual grants and donations.

Responsibility for maintaining and flying the aircraft was transferred to the charity and the aircraft were put onto the UK Civil Aircraft Register. The MOD formally handed over ownership of the airframes to Navy Wings in April 2021. Navy Wings said at the time: "Protecting complex heritage assets like former military aircraft requires the highest standards of airworthiness, operational management and pilot competency for their safe operation and flight. Before taking on responsibility for this most important historic aircraft collection, one of the biggest challenges for Navy Wings has been to become a fully compliant Civil Aviation Authority regulated aircraft operator."

Priceless artefacts

Navy Wings' core collection of aircraft, owned and operated by the Fly Navy Heritage Trust, includes some of the rarest historic aeroplanes in the world. Foremost among them are Swordfish MkI W5856/G-BMGC and MkII LS326/G-AJVH, the only two airworthy examples of the torpedo bomber. Supermarine Seafire XVII SX336/G-KASX, which joined the fleet in 2021, is the only flying Seafire, the naval version of the Spitfire.

Navy Wings' core collection also includes Westland HAS1 Wasp XT420/G-CBUI, built in 1964, which served with 706 and 829 Naval Air Squadron on the ships' flights of HMS *Nubian*, HMS *Hecate*, HMS *Aurora*, HMS *Ajax* and HMS *Hecla*, the last of these during the 1982 Falklands conflict.

Navy Wings aims to fly Sea Fury FB.11 VR930/G-CLNJ again in 2025 after the decision last year to change the aircraft's Bristol Centaurus engine for a Pratt & Whitney R-2800 Double Wasp. The new powerplant was installed in October 2024. This Sea Fury is now like the R2800-equipped Sea Furies flying in the United States. The Royal Navy Historic Flight has had problems with Centaurus engines historically, with three engine failures over the years. In 2024, Navy Wings' chief engineer, Jim Norris, told *Key.Aero*: "Safety really matters and outweighs the need for authenticity."

Hawker Sea Hawk FGA.6 WV908/G-CMFB provides a further contrast in Navy Wings' fleet. The RNHF flew this jet from the early 1980s until 2010 (excepting a seven-year rebuild in 1989-1996). The aircraft was put into dehumidified storage at RAF Shawbury in 2016, awaiting the development and funding of a return-to-flight programme. In 2022, with the funding in place, the aircraft was transported to Yeovilton to begin the process of returning her to flight.

Navy Wings' core collection also includes Stinson Reliant N69745 (FK877), one of 573 Reliants transferred to the Royal Navy under Lend-Lease during World War Two and used extensively by the Fleet Air Arm for navigation training and communications work. There's also North American Harvard G-NWHF, constructed by the Canadian Car and Foundry Company.

Nationwide

Navy Wings participated in more than 60 flying displays and events nationwide in 2024, including Scotland, Northern Ireland and the Channel Islands, reaching an audience of nearly three million people.

ABOVE • *Navy Wings' all-yellow Harvard G-NWHF was constructed by the Canadian Car and Foundry Company.*
SHAUN SCHOFIELD

BELOW • *Swordfish W5856 was built in 1941 by Blackburn Aircraft, hence its 'Blackfish' name.*
SHAUN SCHOFIELD

Naval aircraft obviously seem right at home at seaside airshows and Navy Wings aircraft appeared at many coastal venues during the summer, from Ayr in Scotland and Blackpool and Southport in the northwest to Clacton in Essex and Bournemouth and Torbay on the south coast.

Away from the coast, Navy Wings aeroplanes flew at Duxford and the Shuttleworth Collection at Old Warden. Swordfish W5856 was in the static park for the Goodwood Revival and an event at Sherburn-in-Elmet in North Yorkshire – the latter was particularly poignant, because W5856 and LS326 were among the 1,700 Swordfish built by Blackburn Aircraft at the airfield in 1940-44 (making them 'Blackfish').

Navy Wings participated in Armed Forces Day shows in Bangor, Plymouth and even at the National Arboretum in Staffordshire. They attended Wallop Wheels and Wings in Hampshire and the annual National Air and Space Camp for cadets at RAF Syerston.

Painted in D-Day invasion stripes, Swordfish W5856 was involved in the D-Day 80 commemorations. Navy Wings "stepped in to support the Royal Navy when availability of naval aircraft was severely limited due to the pressure of frontline operations."

'Exceptional'

Navy Wings' contribution to airshows in 2024 also included special flypasts. Taranto Formation brought together Swordfish W5856 and Wasp XT420 with the Black Cats, the Royal Navy Helicopter Display Team and its two Leonardo Wildcat HMA2s. A joint display involved close-formation flypasts, leading into solo displays from the Swordfish and Wasp, then the Black Cats duo.

ABOVE • *Westland Wasp HAS1 is a veteran of the Falklands conflict.*
NIGEL WATSON

BELOW • *Navy Wings' Wasp with a Royal Navy Wildcat HMA2.*
LEE KEUNEKE/ALAMY

There was a special formation at the International Ayr Show – Festival of Flight in Ayr, Scotland, where the Harvard, Reliant and Wasp flew in a formation leading the four Westland/Aérospatiale Gazelle helicopters of the Gazelle Squadron. Previous years have seen combined displays from Swordfish W5856 and the Wasp, and the Wasp and a Wildcat HMA2.

Navy Wings' major involvement in British airshows in 2024 was recognised with the British Air Display Association (BADA) Trophy for 2024. This award, presented annually, honours an individual or organisation's contribution to UK air displays. The BADA Trophy citation read: "Navy Wings' support to air displays around the country with its collection of aircraft has been exceptional in 2024, especially with the Swordfish undertaking some very long cross-country transits in order to participate in as many displays as possible – and that in an aircraft with a 90kt cruise speed!".

Here's a small example of Navy Wings' contribution. On the second weekend of August 2024, Swordfish W5856 displayed at Blackpool early on Saturday afternoon. It immediately departed 'off-slot' (the end of the display) for a show at Compton Abbas in Dorset, several hundred miles south. After overnighting in Dorset, the Swordfish was flown back to Blackpool the following morning. On completing a second display at the Lancashire seaside town, the aircraft once again immediately flew south for a second show at Compton Abbas.

'Golden thread'

While all these transits are relatively short distances in the bigger picture, as the BADA citation noted, the Swordfish's 90kt cruise speed means they still took several hours for the crew to complete – and in the chill of an open-cockpit biplane.

Navy Wings' chief executive officer, Jock Alexander, reflected: "Keeping the history and story of naval aviation in the public eye is a fundamental aim of the charity, and our contribution and reach has been unprecedented. We flew well over 300 hours and the award of the BADA Trophy has been a tremendous accolade to a small charity flying the flag for Britain's great naval aviation heritage."

Alistair McLaren, Navy Wings' Director of Flight Operations, said: "Ex-military aircraft, even more than other types of aircraft, require the highest standards of airworthiness, operational management and pilot competency, and the BADA Trophy recognises the professionalism, expertise and deeply embedded ethos of flight safety of everyone at Navy Wings."

Navy Wings is clear about its objectives, saying in 2019: "These historic aircraft are the golden thread linking the past with current operations and the future. Flying them at airshows and events brings history to life in a dynamic way." ●

Army Flying

Helicopters and aircraft relate the history of UK army aviation

Today, the Army Air Corps – the active combat aviation arm of the British Army – operates Boeing AH-64 Apache attack and Leonardo Wildcat battlefield reconnaissance helicopters.

The AAC was established on September 1, 1957, and its foundation followed decades of close co-operation between the British Army and Royal Air Force units, including operations during World War Two. The history of the 'flying soldiers' – recognisable by their distinctive blue berets – spans fixed-wing and rotary-wing aviation, deployments in Germany, Cyprus, the South Atlantic, Gibraltar and Brunei, and operations in the Persian Gulf, the Balkans and Afghanistan.

The Historic Army Aircraft Flight (HAAF), a registered charity based at Middle Wallop in Hampshire, lists its key aims as heritage and commemoration, public display and engagement, and veterans' support. The HAAF is home to the AAC's historic aircraft, which are flown and supported by volunteers from all walks of life, including former AAC and REME (Royal Electrical and Mechanical Engineers) personnel.

HAAF aircraft are regular visitors to many major airshows and events and can also be seen locally around Hampshire conducting flypasts for occasions such as Remembrance Day.

HAAF background

The HAAF's predecessor was the Army Historic Aircraft Flight (AHAF), formed in 1980 as a non-operational military unit equipped with a single Auster Mk9. The AHAF was established to maintain one example of each aircraft type operated by the Army Air Corps. It was formally recognised by the Army Board in 1990 and is governed by a Military Charter under the guidance of the AAC Regimental Headquarters.

AHAF aircraft were flown by volunteer military aircrew from the serving staff of the Army Aviation Centre at Middle Wallop. By the early 1990s, the AHAF had three fixed-wing types (an Auster, de Havilland Beaver and DH Chipmunk) and three rotary airframes (a Westland Scout, Bell 47 Sioux and Alouette III). It later received Skeeter helicopters and spares.

The AHAF was granted Military Charitable Trust status in 1993 to attract additional income and donations to provide for longer-term investment, but its operations moved in a more dynamic direction in the early 2000s. The flight was relaunched as a six-ship military air display team. By the mid-2000s, its aircraft were appearing in a combined 11-ship routine with the AAC's popular Blue Eagles Display Team, comprising a Lynx AH7 and four Gazelle AH1s.

However, following the incorporation of Army Air Corps operations into Joint Helicopter Command, direct UK Ministry of Defence funding was withdrawn in 2013. The flight was "placed into a state of suspended animation pending further review and likely disposal," according to its website.

It was at this point that George Bacon, who had served with the Army Air Corps Aviation Standards Branch and managed the Blue Eagles and the Army Historic Aircraft Flight, led an ambitious campaign to retain the complete AHAF at Middle Wallop. George's proposal was to incorporate the entire AHAF into a revised version of the existing charitable trust. Following nearly two years of persuasion and lobbying, HQ Army granted permission to gift all the aircraft and spares to a new trust, called the Historic Army Aircraft Flight (HAAF).

ABOVE • *The Army Air Corps received Auster AOP Mk9 XR244 in 1961. It has only ever been based at Middle Wallop.* CHRIS BALLARD

BELOW • *Beaver AL1 G-CICP (ex-XP820) is recognisable by the distinct rasp of its Pratt & Whitney Wasp radial engine.* CHRIS BALLARD

All airframe were transferred from the military to the UK Civil Aviation Authority Civil Aircraft Register.

Today, HAAF operates two Austers (Mk1 G-AHXE and AOP Mk9 G-CICR), de Havilland Canada DHC-2 Beaver AL1 G-CICP, DHC-1 Chipmunk G-CLWK, Westland Scout AH1 G-CIBW, Bell Sioux AH1 G-CICN and Saunders-Roe Skeeter G-SARO.

Austers and Beaver

The Auster entered Army service as the Auster Mk1 in the Air Observation Post (AOP) role. No 651 (AOP) Squadron, based at Old Sarum near Salisbury in Wiltshire, operated them from August 1, 1941.

AOP squadrons, operating different Auster variants (Mk 3/4/5), saw active service throughout World War Two in North Africa, Europe and the Far East. These aircraft were initially flown by pilots from the Royal Artillery, supported by engineers and groundcrew from the Army, RAF and Royal Canadian Air Force

Auster Mk1 G-AHXE (former military registration LB312) was delivered to 651 Squadron on September 24, 1942, but was damaged just over a week later. After repair, she was used by 653 Squadron, then 43 Operational Training Unit, where she served as a trainer for AOP courses until October 1944. Following periods with 3 Tactical Exercise Unit at Aston Down and 234 Squadron, she was 'demobbed' in 1946. She then passed through various civil owners before moving to HAAF in 2021.

Austers evolved through different models. The AOP Mk9 had a more powerful engine, larger wings/flaps, a strengthened undercarriage and a larger cabin. The aircraft was operated by the British Army of the Rhine in Germany and saw active service during the Malayan Emergency in the 1950s and Aden in the early 1960s. The HAAF Auster AOP Mk9, G-CICR, was delivered to the AAC as XR244 in 1961 and has only ever been based at Middle Wallop – after retirement from service in 1981, it became the Army Historic Aircraft Flight's founder aircraft.

HAAF's largest aircraft is Beaver AL1 G-CICP (ex-XP820), recognisable by the distinct rasp of its Pratt & Whitney Wasp radial engine. The Beaver, a medium-range utility aircraft, was used by the AAC in Aden, Malaya and Borneo, later becoming the primary surveillance platform for the Army in Northern Ireland until its replacement by the Britten-Norman Islander in 1989.

The HAAF Beaver was delivered to 11 Flight, 656 Squadron in the Far East, in October 1961, where she remained until June 1967, before returning to 132 Flt RCT at Old Sarum and subsequently to 6 Flt AAC at Netheravon. She was allocated to the historic flight in May 1989 and remains in 'as delivered' condition.

HAAF's other fixed-wing aircraft is Chipmunk G-CLWK (ex-WD325). This was one of the first aircraft to be delivered for army pilot training at Middle Wallop, arriving on October 9, 1957. The 'Chippy' is an aircraft which holds many fond memories for all pilots who all learned to fly in one. At its peak, the School of Army Aviation operated 21 examples, the last of which was only withdrawn from elementary training in 1997.

Scout and Sioux

The Westland Scout was a highly versatile helicopter used for close support, liaison, light freight, medical evacuation, communication, reconnaissance, search and rescue missions and training. It served in Borneo, Aden, Oman, Rhodesia, Northern Ireland, the South Atlantic and with the British Army Over the Rhine. The HAAF's example, G-CIBW (ex-XT626), served from 1963 until the late 1980s, seeing out its service with the Territorial Army at Netheravon.

The Bell 47 first flew on December 8, 1945, and entered service with the US military in 1946. It went on to serve with much success in Korea and Vietnam. The Sioux AH1 entered British Army service in 1964 and was operated as an AOP for the Royal Artillery, as well as for reconnaissance, casualty evacuation, light liaison, underslung loads, operations from ships, pilot training and photography. The type served in the UK, West Germany, the Middle East and the Far East until June 1977. The Historic Army Aircraft Flight's example is XT131, the last Bell 47 to be built by Agusta. She arrived at Middle Wallop in 1964 as a training aircraft and has remained there ever since. ●

ABOVE • *Historic Army Aircraft Flight types, including the Westland Scout, were transferred from the military to the UK Civil Aviation Authority Civil Aircraft Register.* CHRIS BALLARD

BELOW • *The Army Air Corps used the Bell 47 Sioux from 1964 to 1977.* CHRIS BALLARD

Starlings

High-performance displays from two champion aerobatic pilots

The Starlings Aerobatic Team consists of two latest-technology Extra NG aerobatic aircraft flown by team leader Tom Cassells and wingman Michael Pickin. The pair performs close-formation aerobatics, opposition crosses and solo flying in a dynamic, precision routine now widely seen at British airshows, as Tom and Michael bring their years of aerobatic championship experience to display flying.

Background

There are five classes in British Aerobatic Association competition flying: beginner, standard, intermediate, advanced and unlimited.

Yorkshire born-and-bred Tom Cassells, a logistics consultant and aerobatic flying coach, started flying competition aerobatics in 1992 and quickly rose through the different classes. Tom has been the UK Unlimited Class Aerobatic Champion four times, most recently in 2022, and has amassed more than 7,000 flying hours, having flown more than 40 aircraft types.

Michael Pickin has been around flying and aerobatics all his life, inspired by his father, Richard Pickin, a competition and display pilot with decades of experience. Michael started flying as a teenager – he won his first aerobatic competition at just 14 years old – and became the youngest-ever British Advanced National Aerobatic Champion aged 23. He is the youngest person to be awarded a UK Civil Aviation Authority Display Authorisation for display flying. With more than 50 aircraft types in his logbook, his day job is flying the Boeing 737 with TUI Airways.

Tom and Michael both used the Mudry CAP 232 for aerobatic competitions. Tom also displayed his CAP 232 (registered G-IITC) painted in a yellow-and-black chequerboard livery solo at airshows, while Michael built display experience on various types, including his own CAP 232 (G-IIRP).

In 2010, Tom became a founder member with Mark Jefferies of the Global Stars Aerobatic Team, which developed into a four-ship of Extras and CAPs, and displayed extensively overseas, flying in locations such as Bahrain, Dubai, India and Oman. It was, Tom says, "a very nice experience." However, Michael pointed out: "It's quite hard to get four people from different parts of the country, with different jobs, all together to be at the standard you need to be."

Circumstances meant Tom and Michael often flew Global Stars practices together, and eventually the pair felt it logical to form their own display team. They established the Starlings in 2021, by which time Tom had moved on from his CAP 232 to a brand-new Extra NG (G-NGTC). Michael flew his CAP 232 (G-IIRP) with Tom's Extra for the Starlings' first three display seasons in 2021-2023, but replacing his CAP with Extra NG G-IIJM meant the Starlings became an all-Extra team in 2024.

Unlimited Class

British airshows have featured two-ship aerobatic teams for years. There was a Stampe duo, a Zlin 526 pair and the Jubilee Duo of Pitts Specials in the 1970s, as well as the Vixen Two Pitts duo in the early 1980s. The Marlboro Aerobatic Team's red-and-white Pitts performed widely at motor races, carnivals, regattas and family fun days, as well as airshows. Express Newspapers supported a Stampe/Extra EA230 pair in the early 1990s. The Matadors with Sukhoi Su-26s

BELOW • *Precision close formation at Southport in 2024.* NIGEL WATSON

started in 1994. In 1995/1996, TVR Cars backed a Yak-50 team, and in 1995-1997 Rover sponsored an Extra 300 duo from Firebird Aerobatics, the company run by the late Brian Lecomber, a long-time display pilot.

Microlease sponsored the Firebird Extras in the early 2000s, when the flight experience/training company Ultimate High ran an Extra 300 team. Red Bull sponsored the Matadors from 2005 (they later moved from Su-26s to XtremeAir XA41s) and TRIG Avionics supported a Pitts Special duo in the 2010s.

When the Starlings were founded in 2021, both the Matadors and TRIG team had stopped displaying. Michael observed "there was definitely a gap in the market" for a two-ship.

Tom and Michael's Unlimited Class competition aerobatics experience makes the Starlings somewhat different from their many predecessors. Tom pointed out: "Both Michael and I are Unlimited Class pilots. It's not just having a Display Authorisation, it's having Unlimited experience and the rigours of Aresti Unlimited aerobatics at competition level."

Which is demanding flying, to say the least. "When you're doing a competition sequence, the first thing you've got to do is present the flight to the judges," Tom said. Pilots must fly inside a prescribed aerobatic 'box', a 1km^3 block of airspace that's 150-250m from the judges. At Unlimited level, the base height is 100m above the ground. Pilots must fly 13/14 individual figures cleanly and in the optimal position, to ensure the judges can clearly see the shape of each manoeuvre and earn the best possible marks.

The precision flying demanded in competition aerobatic flying means there are relatively few Unlimited pilots. At any one time in the UK, Tom estimates "there might be 100 that do competition aerobatics to the Standard level. I would think 25 of those 100 will go to Intermediate. Out of those 25, five or six go to Advanced, and out of those five or six, you're lucky to get one that goes Unlimited. It's a pretty arduous discipline."

ABOVE • *Positioning to cope with the wind is a challenge at seaside shows, as here at Eastbourne.* ED BROWN/ALAMY

Mentality

"When you do an airshow, people are all applauding," said Tom. "But when you do a competition, people are telling you all the faults they saw. The positioning requirements at Unlimited are as hard as it gets. You must be at the right height – not too high, not too low, not too far to the left, not too far to the right, not too far away, or too close."

Tom thinks the demands of competition aerobatics are "the biggest influence in skill level for display flying." Competition experience helps with the Starlings' displays: "When I'm leading the two-ship I'm a giant firefly – that's how I see it – and I'm positioning that firefly to cope with the wind. We do a lot of seaside shows, and you'll have off-crowd, on-crowd, strong winds. If you're positioning a two-ship, I can't make big alterations to keep the formation spaced nicely."

Michael observed: "You have to be a bit of a perfectionist to even try with competition aerobatics and get to Unlimited. You're never going to be perfect, but you can always try. We try to keep that mentality. Everything can always be improved. I think with both of our competition backgrounds we're always like: 'This could be better'."

Critiquing displays post-show is part of this striving for perfection, and that's easier these days thanks to watching spectators' YouTube videos or playing back a PlanesTV live stream from a show. "There's always a video to watch, so we can always assess how it looked," Tom said. "The other thing about display flying is you need discipline.

STARLINGS

You need to be flying at 70% capacity, you don't want to be flying at 95%.

"The fact that both Michael and I have been Unlimited Aerobatic competitors means the sequences we've flown in the past have been much harder [than airshows]. When we're displaying, we're doing it with a load of spare capacity. The more capacity you have, the more logbooks you'll have."

Tom and Michael are also both accredited Civil Aviation Authority Display Authorised Evaluators, who assess the suitability of a candidate to hold a UK Display Authorisation.

Precision

The Starlings begin their display flying together. "Tom is always leading, I'll be on the right wing, echelon right," Michael explained. "The first part is a mixture of graceful loops, quarter-clovers, wing-overs – or 'slanty loops' as we call them – and barrel-rolls. We try and keep it constantly moving and turning.

"With a two-ship you're limited in what formations you can do, it's either trail or box – where I'm slightly behind and just underneath. It's a mixture of formation changes like that. It then goes into a formation break and a couple of crosses with vertical manoeuvres – stall-turns and humpties. We re-form for a heart just over halfway through the sequence. We then lead into Tom's solo, then a bit of my solo. We finish with a mirror pass, so Tom's inverted and I'll be the right way up."

On the individual solos, Michael said: "We're both flying the same type of aeroplane, so we try and make it that we're not doing exactly the same routine. I'll try and do some of the more Aresti or graceful stuff."

Tumbling manoeuvres are always an eyecatching part of an aerobatic display: "The tumbling looks violent, and certainly the first few times it takes a bit of getting used to but, actually, tumbles only work at slow speed and high power, you're using the gyroscopic forces. The average person would feel some g-force, but it's nothing compared to a high-speed snap roll or even some of the corners you pull around in competition aerobatics."

Tom continued: "We try and do precision tumbles where [the aeroplanes] will do one, or two, or half, or we'll do a frisbee, or from knife-edge we'll flick back up into the vertical, into a torque roll, into a slide. Everything is very precise. There's definite stops to all the figures. I don't like to see people tumbling back through a load of smoke. I like the smoke to be off so people can see the aeroplane. You can have smoke going up, but if you switch the smoke off the crowd can still see the aeroplane.

"It looks pretty if you're doing a torque roll and the wings are level, and it also looks pretty when you do a tailslide and both wings are level, and it does a nice fall through [the smoke]. There's a bit of a nod to precision aerobatics."

Michael explained: "When you see us do a knife-edge spin or a flat spin, we do try to stick to the competition style. It should always finish on an axis. If you don't see a correction afterwards it'll look crisper.

"We want the formation to be neat and tidy, flowing and graceful. We want to do three-quarter rolls like you'd do in a competition, rolls to be in the middle of the line, and [individual] stall turns and rolls to be at the same time."

Extra NG

The Starlings' Extra NG aircraft is the latest evolution in a series of aerobatic monoplanes produced in Germany by Extra Aircraft.

Walter Extra, a successful competition aerobatic pilot, decided in the 1980s to design and build his own aircraft. The line has evolved through EA200, EA230, EA300L, EA300LP, EA330LT, EA330LC, EA330LX and EA330SC. The NG arrived in 2019: "What began as an experimental one-man operation has since grown into an international success story. The Extra brand name has long been synonymous with high standards in providing aerobatic aircraft owners with real next-generation technology. In the new NG we have elevated our excellent workmanship to an even higher level."

The Extra NG features an all-carbon fibre rigid base frame – a first for an aerobatic aircraft – which, Extra Aircraft says, "represents a quantum leap forward." There is a carbon fibre wing assembly with an integrated fuel tank, a carbon monocoque fuselage, a glassfibre landing gear spring, carbon pushrods and a titanium firewall.

ABOVE • *A formation break leads into a couple of crosses with vertical manoeuvres.*
PAUL JOHNSON

BELOW • *A mirror flypast concludes the display.*
CLAIRE HARTLEY VIA THE STARLINGS

ABOVE • *The Starlings bring the precision-flying demands of competition aerobatics to their displays.* CLAIRE HARTLEY VIA THE STARLINGS

Equipped with a six-cylinder 315hp Lycoming AEIO-580-B1A engine with a three-blade MT propeller, the NG has a 400° per second roll rate and is stressed to +/-10G. The company's marketing says: "Improved aerodynamics permit an even higher degree of manoeuvrability and precise handling." The Extra NG is equipped with state-of-the-art Garmin G3X Touch avionics.

Onboard comfort

Extra Aircraft highlights the NG's ergonomically advanced cockpit, designed for maximum pilot comfort. Both front and rear seats are composite, with adjustable forward rudder pedals and differential toe-brakes. The interior is made from carbon and there is leather upholstery.

Michael and Tom certainly notice a difference in comfort from their older aircraft, not least the interior heater. The Extra NG, Michael said, "is everything that, historically, an aerobatic aeroplane wasn't. If you look at the CAP, it's designed purely for aerobatics. In the old Extras and CAPs you'd have to have something wrapped round your neck in the winter, your hands would be freezing and your toes would be absolutely numb after about half-an-hour." Tom said: "Even in summer it's cold In 2024 I positioned a 300L down to Palma and I was absolutely frozen to death. If you've got the in-cockpit heater on it's a pleasant way of moving about."

The Extra NG also offers far superior performance than their earlier aircraft. Tom said: "We're smoking around at 160kts indicated [airspeed], burning what a CAP will burn at 130kts."

Michael noted that a CAP will do 120kts in the cruise and use 50 litres of fuel an hour: "You can get an RV-8 that does 160kts for 32 litres/hour, so [the CAP] is not efficient."

Michael recalled a day during the Starlings' 2024 display season: "We did a show in Cleethorpes in Lincolnshire, then landed at Fenland in Norfolk. We had an hour on the ground and filled up, then put some coals on to fly fast, about 180kts indicated, all the way to Folkestone in Kent. We ran in, on slot, just as we emptied the wing tanks."

However, the Extra NG still had enough fuel not only for the Starlings to display in Folkestone, but also to transit across Kent to Michael's home airfield at Headcorn. None of these sectors – relatively long for a small aircraft – would have been possible in a CAP.

The Starlings' Extras were away in Germany in March/April 2025 for overhaul. They will return to enable the two pilots to undertake a period of pre-season training, mainly in Yorkshire, where Tom is based.

As with all military and civil airshow acts, the Starlings have a set sequence. Looking ahead to the upcoming season, Tom said: "We have slide-outs of looping manoeuvres at 90° in yaw, they look quite nice."

Michael said they are looking at doing more vertical figures in formation and roll-around manoeuvres: "There'll be a few things to keep it different. It's all about trying to keep a good standard." ●

Spitfire

Flying and displaying a high-performance variant of the famous fighter

"The power comes on in a huge surge, deep and smooth. There is a rich throaty growl as I open up the Merlin still further. The acceleration is something I've never experienced before," wrote Geoffrey Wellum in his 2002 memoir *First Light*, recounting his first flight in a Spitfire. Meanwhile, the late Ray Hanna, who displayed Spitfires at airshows for 30 years, once wrote: "No-one can even look at the Spitfire without being awed by the aura of history which will forever surround this fighter and its beautiful crackling Merlin engine." And Czech film director Jan Sverák, who worked with Spitfires on his 2001 wartime drama *Dark Blue World*, said: "When you hear the engine for the first time, you appreciate its awesome power. It feels like attending a Mass."

Whether it's those people on the ground, like Sverák, or those who've flown the aircraft, the Spitfire's Rolls-Royce engine – from the Merlins on early aircraft to the Griffon on later evolutions – always leaves an impression.

The engine is fundamental to the fighter's performance, its sound part of the aeroplane's presence and mystique. Fittingly, Rolls-Royce has its own Spitfire, PR XIX PS853 (registered G-RRGN), based at East Midlands Airport.

Evolution

Rolls-Royce is synonymous with the Spitfire. The company's Merlin and Griffon engines powered the aeroplane from its earliest days and through its continuous development during World War Two.

The first photo-recce Spitfire was the PR IV that arrived in August 1940, then the PR XI, which made its initial flight in August 1941. Rolls-Royce engineers continually worked to improve the Merlin as the Spitfire evolved. In response to a Fleet Air Arm requirement, they developed a larger, more powerful derivative of the engine, the V-12 liquid-cooled Griffon. The first Griffon-engine Spitfire was the Mk XII, followed by the Mk XIV and Mk XVIII.

A photo-recce Spitfire with a higher-performance Griffon was inevitable. The PR XIX was the result – its Griffon 65 or 66 engine developed up to 2,100hp thrust, twice the power of a Spitfire Mk I. Compared to a PR XI, which could do 417mph at around 24,000ft, the PR XIX could reach 460mph and 42,000ft. The PR XIX entered service in May 1944 and 225 examples were built, including PS853. 'Alone, unarmed and unafraid' was the RAF photo-recce squadrons' motto.

Power on tap

Jim Schofield is the chief test pilot at Rolls-Royce and leads the Rolls-Royce Heritage Flight for the 2025 season. He is one of three people who fly PS853 at airshows.

Commenting on the Spitfire's evolution, Jim said: "It was [Spitfire test pilot] Alex Henshaw who said that from the Mk I to the Mk 24 [the last Spitfire variant], one big difference is the weight change. The Mk 24 is the equivalent of a Mk I with 32 passengers and luggage."

Jim reckons earlier Spitfires have the "edge in terms of the balance between power and handling", but he says the PR XIX is "nothing other than delightful." According to him, the Griffon engine makes the Spitfire XIX a very different beast to earlier Spitfires: "It's much more visceral – it definitely feels like 2,000hp that you're in control of, and you fly accordingly.

"You're always gentle with the throttle hand in a Spitfire to make sure these priceless engines last as long as they can between overhauls, but in

ABOVE • Jim Schofield: "It's very hard not to be put in the place of the Spitfire pilots back in the day." JOHN DIBBS VIA ROLLS-ROYCE PLC

the XIX you're just that little bit more conscious that you've got an awful lot of horsepower. You make very smooth throttle inputs so you don't give yourself problems with torque."

Jim spent 20 years in the RAF, during which he became the Ministry of Defence's lead Harrier and Lockheed Martin F-35 test pilot, the Empire Test Pilot School's chief instructor and the wing commander in charge of UK F-35. He's flown more than 115 aircraft types, and he was one of the first pilots to land an F-35 on a ship at night.

Jim said his fast jet background means "you still think in terms of seven or eight miles a minute" when flying, and Spitfire PS853's immense power makes for a rapid speed of events when flying the aeroplane: "At altitude you don't notice the speed per se, but you do notice that you get to places quicker. Your turning points have to be further apart. It shrinks the world, rather than giving you a massive sense of going quicker. Low down, however, is where the world starts whizzing past.

"You have to be careful with airspace. The faster you go, it takes a tiny change in pitch attitude before you're giving rise to massive rates of climb and descent. You need to be careful with height and energy management – but there's so much power on tap, you're never wanting."

'Something I'll never forget'

Jim's father is Carl Schofield, an airline pilot who flew warbirds for the Old Flying Machine Company and The Fighter Collection at Duxford in Cambridgeshire. Jim recounted: "I got to fly in Mustangs and Kittyhawks as a schoolboy. It was inevitable the bug would bite. When I left the RAF in 2016, I was very keen to follow in my father's footsteps and get into the warbird world and start flying these wonderful machines."

In 2015, Jim met Matt Jones from the Goodwood, Sussex-based Boultbee Flight Academy (today known as Spitfires.com), the first company approved for Spitfire passenger flights and the first accredited Spitfire pilot training school.

Jim had the opportunity to fly in a two-seat Spitfire IX: "I'll never forget, I think it was on a Saturday or Sunday, Matt said: 'Jim, what are you doing on Monday? Can you be at Duxford?'. Obviously, I dropped everything and got up there. Matt, most trustingly, sat in the back for my training – except for your first go when they have you sat in the back, so you acclimatise.

"Taking control of a Spitfire for the first time is something I'll never forget – over the Cambridgeshire fields, having got airborne from such a historic airfield as Duxford, and to be handling that wonderful machine. You grow up with all the stories of Spitfire pilots and derring-do – it's quite a poignant moment."

Jim has now spent ten years with Spitfires.com, four of them as its chief pilot. He's flown Spitfires of various marks for many operators and amassed just under 800 flying hours on the type. A new job with Rolls-Royce in 2023 opened up the opportunity to fly

ABOVE • *According to Jim Schofield, "there's so much power on tap, you're never wanting."*
JOHN DIBBS VIA ROLLS-ROYCE PLC

RIGHT • *Rolls-Royce acquired Spitfire XIX PS853 in 1996.*
PAUL R BOLAND/ ROLLS-ROYCE PLC VIA GETTY IMAGES

RIGHT • *Rolls-Royce operates its Spitfire to highlight past engineering achievements and to provide inspiration.*
JONATHAN GREEN/ ROLLS-ROYCE PLC VIA GETTY IMAGES

WWW.KEY.AERO AIRSHOWS OF THE WORLD 2025

SPITFIRE

ROLLS-ROYCE'S SPITFIRE

Spitfire PR XIX PS853 was built by Vickers-Supermarine at their Southampton factory towards the end of 1944. It was one of 79 PR XIXs built at the factory and was delivered to the Central Photographic Reconnaissance Unit at RAF Benson in Oxfordshire on January 13, 1945.

The airframe saw active service with 16 Squadron in sorties over Belgium and Holland, trying to locate possible German V1 and V2 launch sites in northern Europe. After a brief spell with 268 Squadron, she went back to a reformed 16 Squadron at Celle in Germany in September 1945, before going to 29 Maintenance Unit in March 1946.

Having been damaged in a flying incident in January 1949, she sent back to Vickers-Supermarine for repairs, returning to 6 MU in 1950. After time in storage, she went to the Temperature and Humidity of the Upper Air Masses Flight at RAF Woodvale, outside Southport, from 1952 to June 9, 1957. Five days later, along with two other THUM Flight PR XIXs (PM631 and PS915), she was despatched to RAF Biggin Hill in Kent as founding members of the Historic Aircraft Flight. Later, she spent time with the RAF Biggin Hill and RAF North Weald station flights before becoming RAF West Raynham's gate guardian.

After being returned to airworthy condition in 1962, she eventually returned to the Historic Aircraft Flight (HAF) in 1964 and was one of the Spitfires used in the filming of the 1968 film *Battle of Britain*.

Thereafter, PS853 remained part of the HAF – renamed the Battle of Britain Memorial Flight in 1973 – until the Ministry of Defence sold her early in 1995 to raise funds for the rebuilding of Hawker Hurricane IIc PZ865. Following the death of the new owner, Euan English, shortly afterwards, the aircraft was put up for sale again.

Rolls-Royce acquired PS853 in a Sotheby's auction in September 1996. The company operated the aircraft from Bristol/Filton Airport for some years, until moving it to East Midlands Airport, only a short distance away from its headquarters in Derby.

PS853: "They're all delightful aeroplanes, but the XIX is an added dimension."

In their accounts of flying the Spitfire, whether from wartime service or later, many pilots report how it seems the aeroplane is almost an extension of themselves. Barry Sutton, a Battle of Britain veteran, wrote in his poem *Summer of the Firebird*: "Feel it trembling, in gathering power, through my feet, and seat and spine, merging me into its deadliness."

Jim explained why pilots feel such kinship with the Spitfire: "It's a combination of very light controls, and very well harmonised controls. You don't have to put much force in to get the aeroplane to pitch or roll. Because the aeroplane is so well balanced, you don't have to think about overcoming handling issues you might get in a less well-designed aeroplane. It's not only easy to fly in terms of effort, but with training it's easy for an average pilot to fly it well."

Displaying the Spitfire

Jim said the objective of the Rolls-Royce Heritage Flight at East Midlands Airport, which operates Spitfire PS853 and North American AT-6B Harvard KF183/G-CORS, is maintaining historic aeroplanes so "we celebrate our heritage and keep inspiring the public and future engineers."

The flight's Spitfire displays do not include loops, but they do feature a combination of close passes, graceful barrel rolls and half-Cuban eights, which involve pulling up as for a loop before rolling off the top. Jim especially enjoys the last of these manoeuvres: "You've got five-eighths of a loop, the glorious conversion of speed to height in the first half, then you can show the aircraft's roll rate and gracefully recover to the same height you started at."

Rolls-Royce has a set Spitfire display routine, although Jim points out there is flexibility to optimise the sequence based on the shape of a display venue to best show the aircraft to the crowd: "There could be trees that mean you need to be flying higher. You might need to be on the B axis descending towards the crowd [the A axis is the display line left-to-right from the crowd's perspective] rather than holding it level from a lower height. I'll tailor it to try and make it look good. That means it's slightly different at every venue from my perspective.

"Generally I start off with the high-energy manoeuvres. About halfway through I tend to come back on the power a bit and fly more flypasts. I've learnt at venues like Shuttleworth [Old Warden Aerodrome, Bedfordshire] that if you spend the whole display doing aerobatics, photographers see it just as pilots enjoying themselves! [Photographers] like lower, more stable flypasts, ideally with the trees or the [Old Warden airfield] shed in the background to give a sense of perspective and depth. I try to cater to that."

Jim notes there is always a planned sequence for a given day, but there is flexibility to optimise a display given the prevailing weather conditions – the cloud base, for instance, might be lower at one end of a display line than at the

BELOW • *Rolls-Royce Spitfire displays include close passes and graceful barrel rolls, as here at Eastbourne in 2024.*
ED BROWN/ALAMY

other. Adjusting a display in this way, accounting for "where the sun is, where the wind is and what I think the crowd want to see," while keeping everything safe and within the air display regulations, is part of the challenge of airshow flying.

Presumably, displaying a Spitfire at an airshow is very satisfying? Jim said: "It always puts a smile on your face, but you are professionally displaying an aircraft within multiple parameters for safety and the airshow rules. That's hard work but obviously great fun, and after you've done that safely and successfully, having gracefully displayed the aeroplane well within its capabilities, you get a secondary sense of satisfaction when the aircraft is back in the hangar and you're driving home.

"Clearly, it's such an amazing machine to fly – you'd have to be half-dead not to get a thrill out of that."

Inspiration

Rolls-Royce has a long tradition of having a company Spitfire, according to Jim: "We operated a Mk XIV Spitfire from 1948, initially as a testbed, then as a display aircraft." (This was RM689, sadly lost in a June 1992 accident.) "We acquired the Mk XIX in the 1990s. It's seen as very important within Rolls-Royce to highlight the amazing engineering that went on in the 1930s and 1940s to help Britain win the war. We shouldn't underestimate the impact on youngsters of seeing these wonderful British icons being flown gracefully at an airshow, and what that does to inspire them into a career in engineering, or aviation in general.

"We feel that responsibility, and to that end, we're always displaying the aircraft, we're never displaying us. That's a great principle – it's always about the aeroplane."

In 2025, the Rolls-Royce Heritage Flight plans to take Spitfire PS853 to the larger UK flying events, naturally including some of the UK's best-attended airshows at the seaside.

"You don't need to be an engineer to understand the nation holds the Spitfire very close to its heart. It's always a surprise to me – but also a great joy – that 80 years later that's still the case. Whenever you land somewhere, and you're talking to the public, it's very evident that everybody holds the Spitfire in such high regard. It's such a great privilege to be given the opportunity to fly the aircraft, demonstrate it, and help inspire. We've all seen the films of Spitfires flying through lofty turrets of cumulus clouds, and spotting roving fighters. It's such an evocative picture in all of our minds that when you are flying a Spitfire, and there are clouds around, it's very hard not to be put in the place of the Spitfire pilots back in the day." ●

ABOVE • *PS853's mighty 2,000hp Rolls-Royce Griffon engine undergoing annual maintenance.* ROLLS-ROYCE IMAGE RESOURCE

BELOW • *Spitfire PS853 in the skies above Warwickshire.* JONATHAN GREEN/ROLLS-ROYCE PLC VIA GETTY IMAGES

DISPLAY TEAMS

The Red Arrows' first display season with the Hawk T1 was 1980, closer in time to the Battle of Britain in 1940 than it is to today. The squadron is the last RAF Hawk T1 unit. In January 2025, the Conservative MP Ben Obese-Jacty submitted a written question to the UK Ministry of Defence (MOD) about the fatigue life on Red Arrows Hawks. A table provided in response by the MOD detailed the percentage of the fatigue index remaining on the unit's aircraft – the 14 Hawks assigned to the primary fleet and 12 other aircraft in a sustainment fleet.

In the primary fleet, one Hawk (XX242) has used 94.65% of its fatigue index. Most other jets have used 80-88%, although the figure for one aircraft (XX295) is lower at 68.63%. The MOD's data showed the fatigue index values for the 12 Hawks in the sustainment fleet are in the 70-79% range, with the exceptions of XX284 (68.31%) and XX301 (68.98%). A written statement from UK defence secretary, Maria Eagle, said: "Across all airframes we have retained more than sufficient overall remaining available fatigue life to ensure all Red Arrows tasking[s] until 2030 as planned." The UK's latest Strategic Defence Review, under way at the time of writing and due to report this year, will likely include any further decisions about the Red Arrows' longer-term future.

ABOVE • *The RAF roundel and the UK flag on the Red Arrows' aircraft reflect the team's roles of promoting the air force and country.* UK MINISTRY OF DEFENCE/CROWN COPYRIGHT 2024

BELOW • *The US Navy Blue Angels and US Air Force Thunderbirds in a Super Delta formation over Naval Air Facility El Centro in 2021.* MASS COMMUNICATION SPECIALIST 2ND CLASS CODY HENDRIX/US NAVY

Unfortunately, an underlying issue confronts the longer-established European display teams: the era of plentiful aircraft, people and budgets when many air forces formed them years ago simply doesn't exist today. Pierre-Alain Antoine, who commanded the Patrouille de France in 1990-92, noted to *Aviation News* in 2023 that back when he began his career in the 1960s, the French Air Force had more than 500 frontline fighters and 100,000 personnel; the numbers today are a third of those figures. Pierre-Alain observed: "The price of an aerobatic team is very high [and] we continue to pay a lot. What will be the decision now, when we have a very small air force?"

According to *Le Matin*, the Patrouille Suisse F-5s cost 40 million Swiss francs a year to operate and the bill will increase to around 80 million Swiss francs to maintain the 12 aircraft beyond 2027. Over the years, several air arms have axed teams to cut costs. The Belgian Air Force disbanded Diables Rouge (Red Devils) with Fouga Magisters in 1977, as did the Austrian Air Force Karo As (Ace of Diamonds) with Saab 105OEs in 1984. The Slovak Air Force Biele Albatrosy (White Albatross) with Aero L-39C Albatros stopped flying in 2004, while the Flygvapnet (Swedish Air Force) disbanded Team 60 with Saab SK 60s in 2008.

State symbol

Today's demands on defence budgets and public finances might suggest the

display teams age could fade away, but various teams re-equipping shows this isn't the case.

Pierre-Alain Antoine told *Aviation News* in 2023 that a national display team "is a state symbol – and more", with a role to play in national life: "For the Platinum Jubilee of The Queen or for the Coronation of King Charles III it was impossible to imagine that there would be no overflight of Buckingham Palace by the Red Arrows. In France, it is impossible to imagine an overflight of the Champs-Elysée on Bastille Day without the Patrouille de France."

Here's what the Indian Air Force said of its Surya Kiran Aerobatic Team (SKAT), equipped with the BAE Systems Hawk 132 Advanced Jet Trainer, in the brochure for the Aero India show in February 2025: "SKAT not only serves as a symbol of national pride but also demonstrates the IAF's operational capabilities and commitment to excellence. Their performances inspire young aviators and instil a sense of patriotism among spectators."

The Spanish news agency Europa Press quoted Spain's defence minister, Margarita Robles, commenting in March 2025 about Patrulla Àguila moving to the PC-21: "The great celebrations of this country cannot be understood without the team."

ABOVE • *The Royal Australian Air Force Roulettes have operated Pilatus PC-21s since 2021.* LACW PARIS RIGNEY/ROYAL AUSTRALIAN AIR FORCE

BELOW • *An extensive global tour for the Republic of Korea Air Force Black Eagles in 2022/23 culminated in displays at the Australian International Airshow at Avalon.* LACW ANNIKA SMIT/ROYAL AUSTRALIAN AIR FORCE

Teams add a flourish to formal occasions or an added dimension to major national events. The Red Arrows fly along The Mall in central London after Trooping the Colour each June, and over the Tyne Bridge in Newcastle during the Great North Run.

Frecce Tricolori lays down Italy's national colours over Monza before the Italian Grand Prix. Patrouille Suisse sometimes fly over the Alps during championship skiing events. The Royal New Zealand Air Force Black Falcons team of Beechcraft T-6C Texan II aircraft perform at national triathlons and motor racing events.

Teams express national identity with their paint schemes, trailing the national colours if their aircraft are suitably equipped – and sometimes with manoeuvres they perform. The Fursan Al Emarat display finale, which is called DNA, is an example. This manoeuvre interprets the UAE flag: two jets corkscrew with red smoke around the other five trailing black, green and white. The manoeuvre is flown relatively slowly, so the

DISPLAY TEAMS

LEFT • *Nations with smaller defence budgets still want a display team. Here are the Royal Norwegian Air Force Yellow Sparrows at RIAT 2024.* NIGEL WATSON

aircraft engines run hotter, leaving thick smoke trails.

Frecce Tricolori's finale, Alona, creates an enormous curve of vivid smoke often described as the world's largest Italian flag; Luciano Pavarotti sings *Nessun Dorma* on the PA system as they perform it. South Korea's Black Eagles draw the country's Taegeuk flag in favourable weather conditions. Los Halcones put Chile's five-point star in the sky.

Patrouille Suisse formations have included Federer, Toblerone and Milking Stool. Their PC-7 Team compatriots fly the Matterhorn Split and a formation called Pilatus honouring the mountain after which the aircraft company is named. Both Swiss teams perform a 'tunnel' manoeuvre – one aircraft flies through a gap in a triangle formed by the others – representing the Gotthard Tunnel beneath the Alps to Italy.

'The pursuit of beauty'

Display teams are part of the national furniture and flying the flag for their home country on the international stage is part of why they exist. There's a long tradition here. As far back as the 1930s, Britain, Czechoslovakia, Germany, France, Italy and Switzerland routinely sent national teams to the annual Meeting Aéronautique International in Zurich. An RAF de Havilland Vampire display team from 54 Squadron was sent to perform in Canada and the United States in 1948, becoming the first jet aircraft formation to fly across the Atlantic Ocean. The Royal Jordanian Falcons were set up in 1976 specifically to boost Jordan's image overseas. In the Aero India 2025 brochure, the Indian Air Force says SKAT represents "India's aviation prowess on the world stage."

Lieutenant Colonel Massimiliano Salvatore, the current Frecce Tricolori commanding officer, wrote in the team's 2024 brochure that the Frecce is "a symbol of Italianess". The team, he wrote, "added the pursuit of beauty and harmony that have always been characteristic of the Italian style of doing things – the 'made in Italy' that is recognised and appreciated worldwide."

Teams might often support wider national trade/industry promotional efforts. The Red Arrows have long had

BELOW • *Fursan Al Emarat flies the DNA, manoeuvre drawing the United Arab Emirates flag at the 2021 Dubai Airshow.* JEAN-VINCENT RAYMONDON/AIRBUS

ABOVE • *The Royal Jordanian Falcons were established specifically to serve as roving ambassadors for their home country.*
FILIP MODZREJEWSKI

twin roles of acting as ambassadors both for the RAF and the UK. Back in June 1965, only six weeks after their public debut, they were sent to perform at the year's largest industry event, the Paris Air Show at Le Bourget. The team still regularly tours the Middle East, North America and the Far East.

Several Middle East/Asia-Pacific teams have noticeably sped up the pace of their ambassadorial activity on the world stage in recent years. The Saudi Hawks in 2023 performed at the Royal International Air Tattoo (RIAT) and at shows in Salon de Provence (France), Sanicole (Belgium), Tanagra (Greece) and Zeltweg (Austria). They returned to RIAT and Tanagra in 2024. Fursan Al Emarat has performed recently in Kuwait, Malaysia, Morocco, Saudi Arabia, Slovakia, Switzerland, Turkey and the UK.

South Korea's Black Eagles undertook an extensive world tour in 2022/2023. They performed in the UK at Southport and RIAT, before visiting Poland, Slovakia, Croatia, Azerbaijan, Egypt, the UAE, Pakistan, Thailand, Malaysia and Vietnam on their route home, before heading to the tour's final destination, Avalon, for the Australian International Airshow. Early in 2024 they went to the Singapore Airshow.

'Must-have'

Teams' visual spectacle can leave a lasting impression. This author, for instance, can recall from childhood seeing the Frecce Tricolori's vibrant green, white and red smoke above RAF Fairford, as well as the red-and-white undersides of the Patrouille Suisse Hunters against the grey skies at an airshow in northern Britain.

The longer-established teams provide a certain sense of constancy as the years go by. Parents and grandparents watching a Red Arrows display in 2025, for example, may well have seen the same spectacle – red jets trailing smoke – when they were children themselves. Few other things in national life endure in quite the same way.

Tim Prince is Honorary Vice-Patron of RIAT and the RAF Charitable Trust, who founded the event with the late Paul Bowen in the early 1970s. Multiple national teams performing at each year's Tattoo is a longstanding aspect of RIAT, the world's largest annual military airshow. Tim told *Aviation News* in 2023: "There were times in the 1980s and 1990s when we were becoming oversubscribed and it became necessary to gently persuade some teams to only participate on alternate years, desperately endeavouring to avoid causing diplomatic offence!".

Despite budgetary/operational pressures making air forces selective about airshow participation these days, the re-equipment efforts – or continuing with older aircraft – shows the spirit remains very strong worldwide to have a national display team. Tellingly, even countries with relatively small air forces and modest defence budgets maintain teams. The Royal Norwegian Air Force has the Yellow Sparrows with the Saab MFI-15 Safari, and the Croatian Air Force Wings of Storm with Pilatus PC-9Ms.

In 2011, the Royal New Zealand Air Force formed its Black Falcons with T-6Cs and the Belgian Air Force revived the Diables Rouge name for a team of four SIAI-Marchetti SF260 trainers although this team will disband this year. The Irish Air Corps revived the Silver Swallows with PC-9Ms in 2022.

Even as it sealed the fate of the Patrouille Suisse F-5s, the Swiss Federal Council said it wanted a Swiss national team to continue. *Le Matin* reported that the Swiss Federal Department of Defence, Civil Protection and Sport is currently "examining the possibility of continuing it with another type of aircraft".

Tim Prince reflected to *Aviation News*: "I suspect the main reason for [teams'] longevity is their importance to their owners. Their value and reach make them a must-have'." ●

THE DESTINATION FOR AVIATION ENTHUSIASTS

KEY Publishing

Visit us today and discover all our publications

Combat Aircraft Journal is renowned for being America's best-selling military aviation magazine.

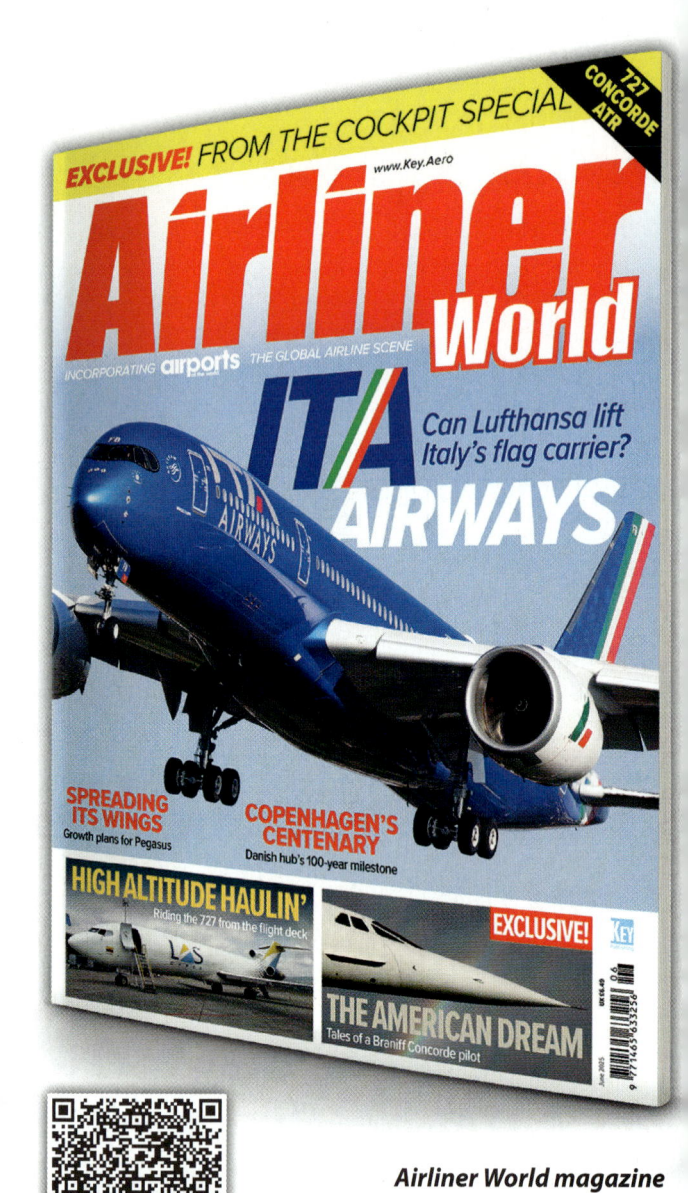

Airliner World magazine is the biggest-selling commercial aviation magazine in the world.

SIMPLY SCAN THE QR CODE OF YOUR FAVOURITE TITLE ABOVE TO FIND OUT MORE!

Order from our online shop...

shop.keypublishing.com

Call +44 (0)1780 480404 *(Mon to Fri 9am - 5.30pm GMT)*

SUBSCRIBE TODAY!

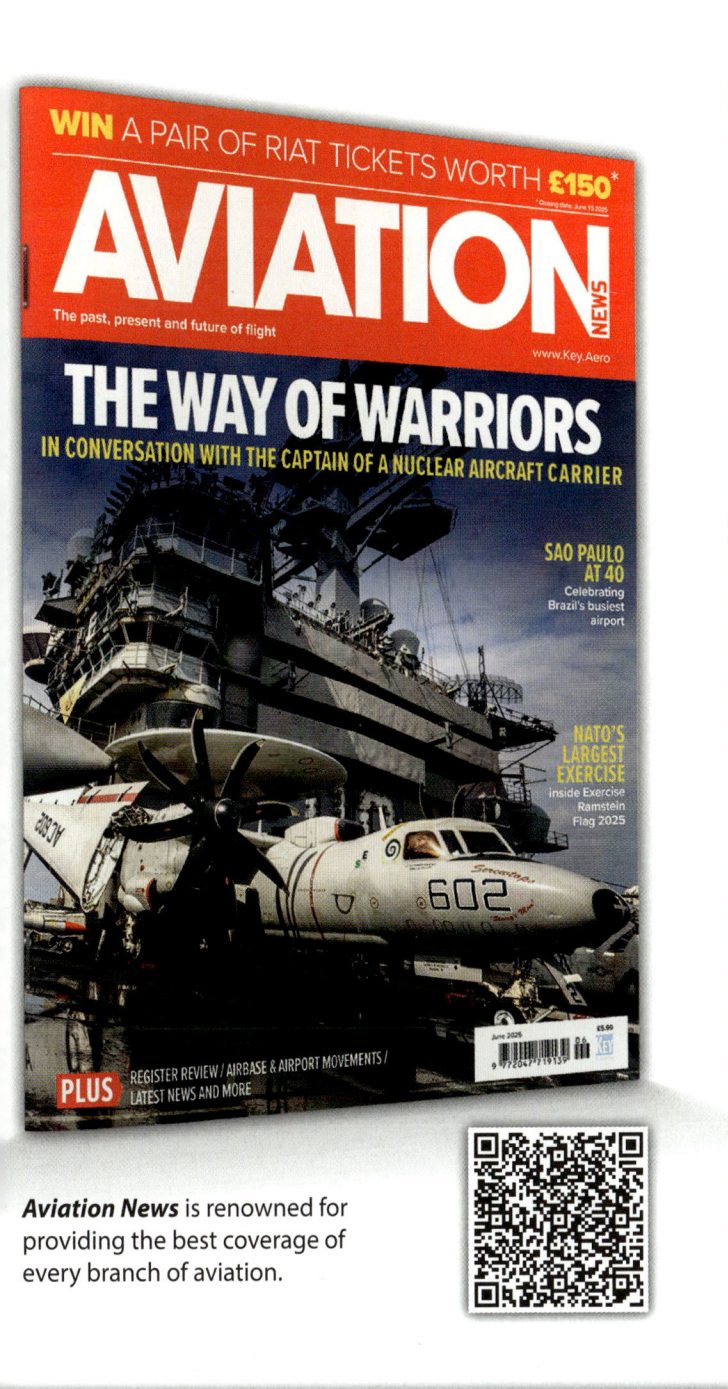

Aviation News is renowned for providing the best coverage of every branch of aviation.

Airforces Monthly is devoted to modern military aircraft and their air arms.

/collections/subscriptions

*Free 2nd class P&P on BFPO orders. Overseas charges apply.

WINGWALKING

Wingwalking

Display smoke, colour, noise and aerial acrobatics recall the flying circus era

The 1920s were the years of fun: flappers, jazz, Art Deco and Hollywood stardust starting to shine. Aeroplanes were still relatively new, so airshows generated enormous curiosity and wonder. Flying circuses and wingwalking added to the excitement.

Back then, wingwalking was quite literally just that – men and women walked along and between the wings (and moved between aeroplanes) in flight. With no parachute or safety wires, these feats often led to tragedy. Wingwalking was banned in 1933 and it was revived only decades later with new safety equipment.

AeroSuperBatics

Flying immaculate Boeing Stearman biplanes, AeroSuperBatics operates the world's only formation wingwalking display team from the picturesque private airfield of Rendcomb in Gloucestershire.

Currently unsponsored and flying as the AeroSuperBatics Wingwalkers, you may recall their earlier guises as the Yugo Cars Flying Circus, Cadbury's Crunchie Flying Circus, Utterly Butterly Barnstormers, Team Guinot and the Breitling Wingwalkers.

Established by Vic Norman, AeroSuperBatics celebrated its 40th anniversary in 2024. The team displays in front of six million people a year. It has performed in 20 countries, and regularly visits events in Europe, Asia and the Middle East.

It's easy to see why the team has been around for so long. The wingwalking, the Stearman's rasping 450hp Pratt & Whitney radial engines and the plumes of white smoke (created using environmentally-friendly AeroShell Ondina smoke oil) creates what people want on a day out at an airshow: spectacle.

Facing wind speeds of up to 160mph, the team's professional wingwalkers are securely strapped into a harness on the top wing of the Stearmans. As the pilots fly close formation flypasts and aerobatics, the girls perform acrobatics using a specially made swivelling rig that enables them to lie on their sides, parallel with the wing, and perform handstands.

Being a wingwalker

Emma Broadbent is one of AeroSuperBatics' current professional wingwalkers. She especially likes doing a handstand while the Stearman flies a barrel roll. "When the aeroplane is upside down, we're the right way up," she pointed out. "It's amazing – you feel like you're holding up an aeroplane and you're weightless as well. That's really cool.

"Towards the end of the routine is the real fun bit. We take the harness off. We're attached with a secondary safety wire – we're never not attached to the aeroplane – but we hope to show we're climbing freely around. We'll sit on the leading edge with our arm in front of us at 90 knots [this manoeuvre is called the Goose]. We'll then climb under the rigs and put a foot on the cockpit in front of the glass of the pilot."

The wingwalkers place their foot into an area the size of a beermat to perform another manoeuvre called the reverse Goose. On the final pass, the girls perform a ballet pose called an Arabesque: "This requires you to get your leg above your head. One foot is suspended on this little size of a beermat, and we've got our other leg in the air above performing the splits whilst holding on. It's really challenging and you feel really good once you've done it."

Professional wingwalking obviously requires huge physical strength and

BELOW • *The Aerosuperbatics Wingwalkers 'B' break during an evening display at Ayr in Scotland in September 2024.*
PAUL JOHNSON

ABOVE • *In the Arabesque, the wingwalkers place a foot on an area the size of a beermat while performing the splits.*
PAUL JOHNSON

dexterity. Emma said: "The most surprising thing when you get on the wing, and you're doing it at display speed, is quite how fast you're going, and quite how forceful the wind is on your body. It takes a little while to get your head around how you're going to get your leg above your head while you're travelling at 100mph and still look graceful. When I first did it, I thought 'How on Earth am I going to do this and make it look good?', but over time you just practice, and get used to it."

Professional wingwalkers must "have some experience of performing and doing strength and mobility," Emma pointed out. Work or interests in dancing or gymnastics are typical; Emma's colleague Kirsten Pobjoy was once a circus trapeze artist. Emma said: "That's the sort of background you need to have, because what we do requires you to climb up and down the aeroplane, and all these movements have to happen in the air, while being super safety conscious."

A head for heights and a taste for adventure and adrenaline are obviously essential. Emma also enjoys kitesurfing, skydiving and marathon running, and she's been cage-diving with sharks.

Just as there are lead/formation pilots in a display team, so there are lead/formation wingwalkers. "The professional wingwalkers' main aim is to match each other," Emma said. "For me, as the formation wingwalker, my role is to watch Kirsten carefully, even though It's very difficult to do that sometimes, because we're underneath the other aeroplane – all I can see is a few fingers.

"We have certain hand signals, so I know which move it's going to be, but having done the routine so many times now – and we have a set choreographed piece – I can anticipate what's coming next."

Emma and Kirsten have been wingwalkers since 2021 and 2018 respectively, but Emma emphasised: "On days where the conditions are a bit challenging, or we're required to improvise or change the routine, I need to be really focused." There's a lot of mental preparation involved and ongoing training in the Rendcomb hangar. Any new wingwalker will undergo extensive ground training, learning how to climb up and down the aeroplane, before they go flying.

Emma said it's impossible to narrow down a favourite display venue, although she enjoys the UK seaside shows "and one of most beautiful places we've performed in is Sligo in Ireland."

Inevitably, the team must perform in often-changeable British summer weather, which for a wingwalker sometimes means directly facing into 100mph driving rain. "You wouldn't wish it on your worst enemy, it's really painful!" Emma said. "But as long as it's not raining, we're likely to enjoy every display."

Emma said people can try wingwalking for themselves with AeroSuperBatics: "It's amazing, and It's something we hope everyone can do. Those that are fit to fly and meet our minimum requirements are more than welcome to come and experience wingwalking with our professional team." (Visit www.aerosuperbatics.com to find out more.)

Different dimension

AeroSuperBatics' chief pilot Dave Barrell has been flying with the team since 2007: "The Stearman was built as a training aircraft and, as a result, they deliberately made it a challenge to fly. When you're sitting in the cockpit on the ground you can't see anything in front of you at all because of the way the aircraft sits on its tail. When you're taxiing you need to weave from side to side so you always clear your nose."

WINGWALKING

LEFT • *Emma Broadbent is one of Aerosuperbatics' current wingwalkers.*
EMMA BROADBENT

The wings, struts and wires limit the view in flight: "When we're transiting, we generally weave slightly to clear our nose so we know what's in front of us. Coming in to land, we try to do curved approaches or something that's close to the runway – a short circuit with a short base leg and a short final – just so you can see the runway. A crosswind makes it even more of a challenge."

Dave really enjoys Stearman flying despite its challenges: "It's got rod controls, not cables. As soon as you use the stick, the aeroplane moves around. It's a very pilot-friendly aeroplane. It's open cockpit, you're not enclosed. You feel more connected with the air. It's noisy, and its cold, but you just feel a whole different dimension.

"Anywhere you land, the aircraft attracts a lot of attention. We're flying vintage machines and people don't really get to see them very often. I feel very privileged to be able to bring that kind of technology to people."

The AeroSuperBatics Wingwalkers display begins with a formation loop, before the aeroplanes position onto the 'B' axis, the display line extending out from crowd centre (the 'A' axis is the display line running from left to right parallel with the crowd line).

There's an opposition break on the 'B' axis (the line heading straight towards the crowd), where the aeroplanes cross paths as they approach the crowd. There are then several opposition manoeuvres, before the aeroplanes rejoin for a synchronised barrel roll and close formation passes.

Display flying

Dave explained how they developed their displays: "We ran the same routine for many years. We used to do a loop and then two formation passes. The feedback from the public was that that was a bit boring, so we decided we'd do a loop in formation and then go straight into the 'B' break.

"We used to fly an opposition bump, a 45 cross and then a head-to-head rejoin. People said they found those quite exciting, so we put in another two. As we speak, myself and a couple of the other pilots are working on moving it up even more. We've got other things in the pipeline to make it even more exciting."

Dave described some of the challenges in display flying: "The easiest display is with no wind – we can fly low and close and we don't have to compensate for anything – but obviously that doesn't always happen! For example, at Blackpool in 2024, we had a north-westerly, so we were getting blown onto the crowd and getting blown south as well.

"When we do opposition manoeuvres with two aircraft, we want to do crosses in the middle of the crowd. It's all about mathematics and calculation, whereby the guy in the aircraft that's going into wind counts one second for every five knots of wind component. So if there's a southerly 10kt wind blowing down the coast at Blackpool, then the guy that's travelling southbound in the display would roll out onto a northerly heading and count to two, then turn the aircraft in, whereas the other guy would turn immediately.

"If you're watching both aircraft, you'll see one guy turn quite sharply, and the other guy will keep going. Some people will think 'What's he doing?'. He's biting into the wind, because as soon as he turns and takes the tailwind, he's travelling downwind very quickly. You have to put in a timing correction.

"In the display, you might hear us on the radio say something like 'Four for you, five for you, six for you'. That's us recalculating how much time correction to give. It might be it was zero, we might be in the right position, but generally the higher you go, the stronger the wind. If the wind is 10kts on the surface, it might be 20kts at 1,000ft, so it can be quite difficult to sometimes work out how much drift we've got.

"As leader, as well as fly the aircraft, I have to consider my wingman, which is all about using my power to get him to stay where he should be – for example, turning left I have to reduce power, turning right I have to increase power.

BELOW • *A swivelling rig enables Aerosuperbatics' wingwalkers to lie on their sides and perform handstands.* NIGEL WATSON

I have to fly my aeroplane as if I'm in his cockpit. It's all done by sighting. The other guy is watching me, he's not watching the display site at all. I need to call him to tell him what to do to make the display remain in the centre."

Weightless

The wingwalkers, of course, are a further consideration for the pilots. What effect on flying the Stearman do they have as they move around the aeroplanes?

Dave noted that the girls are sometimes on the wing at some displays when the team takes off, but at other venues they sit in the front cockpit before climbing up onto the wing: "For example, at Eastbourne we could be travelling with them for 15 minutes down the coast with them in the front seat. When we get to the hold, we have to slow the aircraft down to 75-80mph and then get them to climb up onto the wing. As soon as they climb out of the cockpit into the airflow, the aeroplane takes drag and slows down. You immediately have to trim the aeroplane and increase power to keep it at flying speed."

The girls indicate to the pilots by hand signal that they're safety locked into the harnesses. The opening manoeuvre, the formation loop, starts at 1,000ft.

"We need the speed in the dive to get over the top of the loop," Dave said. "As soon as the aircraft goes vertical with the girl on the wing it starts slowing down – you could liken it to flying an aircraft with the gear/flaps down. Upside down you're quite slow and it's very difficult to stay in formation. We try to go in with plenty of speed to carry us over the top.

ABOVE • *The Scandinavian Airshow team use a Grumman Ag Cat. Here they are displaying at the 2023 Hunter Valley Airshow in Australia.*
SGT GLEN MCCARTHY/ AUSTRALIAN DEFENCE FORCE

"For the girls, they're going in [to the loop] at 150mph and 4G, then over the top of the loop it's almost weightless and very slow, 60mph, but then within a few seconds we're at 160mph – and, of course, they have to be smiling and waving."

During the opposition manoeuvres, some speeds are high, and some speeds are low. All the while, the girls change position as they perform their acrobatics: "Occasionally we'll glance up to make sure they're OK – generally, they are.

"At the end, when they start climbing over the aircraft, we have to fly the aircraft below 100mph. The girls are very good. We do a lot of training, and a lot of safety-related training. We always do a walk-through, so everyone knows exactly what they're doing."

Emma said: "The thing I enjoy the most is the team, and that we get to do this extraordinary job together. Being able to fly around together and perform – it feels really special to call it a job. Climbing around on an aeroplane – it's very cool to say you're used to doing that!

"We're super-friendly people that are passionate about flying. We just love to see everyone there [at airshows] and have chats with them. We absolutely love what we do – it's a very special thing."

Catwalk

The Scandinavian Airshow team in Sweden is another European wingwalking display act, using a single specially modified Grumman G-164 Ag Cat (SE-KXR) in a yellow/black livery, in an act called Catwalk. Team leader, and Ag Cat pilot, Jacob Hollander, explained: "We have two wingwalkers, one on the top wing and one on the bottom wing."

The team calls its wingwalkers the Skycats. As with AeroSuperBatics in the UK (and 46 Aviation, see p.46-47), the Skycats perform a set programme of acrobatic moves during the display. "We don't change anything in the display – we haven't since 2011 – that makes it easy for the pilot and the Skycats," Jacob said.

A standard operating procedure for the team is for its wingwalkers to be skydivers and hold a skydiving licence or to have done wind-tunnel training. Jacob explained: "Skydivers are used to moving in the air. For us it works very well – they have a basic knowledge of how to handle the wind." Planning, rehearsals and briefing are still of the highest importance, of course.

How do the wingwalkers affect the flight of the big, chunky Ag Cat? Jacob revealed: "You have [to use] more rudder. When they're sitting on the wings, they disturb the laminar flow, the lift over the wings. You have to compensate for it, especially if you're at low speed. When they go up and do other manoeuvres, like the Super Cat – so they look like Superman – you can really feel it."

Jacob will notice when one of the wingwalkers moves from the top wing down to the lower wing, leaving both wingwalkers on the lower wings, with one on each side of the fuselage: "When they start to move out, you have some buffeting on the stabiliser. It's not a big thing, but you can feel the turbulence around the tail. But we've done this for a long time now, so you don't really think about it". ✈

WINGWALKING

Wingwalker Danielle

Wingwalker Danielle from 46 Aviation in Switzerland is the wingwalking act from the husband-and-wife team of Emiliano and Danielle Del Bueno using a Boeing Stearman. *Airshows of the World 2025* asked her about her background.

Could you introduce yourself to us?
"I'm Danielle Del Buono, a professional wingwalker for 46 Aviation Classics. My husband Emiliano is the pilot and CEO and Swiss Unlimited Aerobatic Champion. 46 Aviation Classics is based in Sion, Switzerland. We perform the original style of wingwalking."

How did you get into wingwalking?
"My mother and father took me to a local airshow at six years old. I was fascinated by the fantastic flying machines, but mostly by the wingwalking act. The wingwalking grabbed my heart, and I just knew from then on: 'That's what I'm gonna do when I grow up!'. I couldn't believe what I was seeing – there was a person on the top wing of a biplane and I couldn't take my eyes off the show!

"In 2007, when I was 18 years old, I discovered AeroSuperBatics were looking for a new wingwalker. It was advertised in my local newspaper. After a few interviews and a flying audition, I was lucky enough to get the job: I became a professional wingwalker.

"I was extremely excited and felt very lucky to have been given the opportunity, since it had been a childhood dream. I worked with them for nine years. It was a great experience, and I made lifelong friends and many happy memories.

"In 2014, whilst participating at Air14 Airshow in Payerne, Switzerland, I met and fell in love with Emiliano Del Buono. Eventually I moved to Switzerland and we got married, and now we have two children and three dogs together."

Tell us about your act.
"We had the opportunity to fly together on a Stearman operated by 46 Aviation. The aircraft had all the necessary modifications and we had the experience. With Emiliano's taildragger, aerobatic and warbird flying experience, combined with my airshow wingwalking knowledge, we were able to design an entertaining flying sequence. We've performed at airshows together since 2016. I had the freedom to walk in between the wings and do the original style of wingwalking – walking the wings, stepping over the wires, dancing and gliding gracefully on my sky horse.

"The first time I did this, it felt incredible! I started in the front cockpit and looked in the mirror at my pilot/ husband, waiting for him to give me the 'thumbs up' to climb out. I proceeded to undo my cockpit straps and tidy them away carefully. I stood up on the seat and took a deep breath as I made my first step out on to the wing. The force of the wind was immense, and I could feel the propwash fight against me. I knew it was going to be tough and take a lot of strength, but I felt more determined than ever. I used the wires to hold on to and carefully stepped out further, placing my feet only on the ribs of the wing, navigating myself towards the javelin.

"I lay across the javelin, my position for the loop. It's a great way to view the world go around. I felt so free! Also, it was kind of romantic, walking out on the wing while my husband flies me!".

Are you ever nervous when stepping out of your seat and on top of the wing?
"I feel slightly nervous and have a feeling of butterflies before every flight, even now, but I believe this is a good thing as it helps me to focus, concentrate and consider safety carefully."

How much training is required to go on top of the wing and perform?
"I had to practice for weeks with the aeroplane just on the ground, tracing my steps and preparing everything accurately. I walk out to the very far edges of the wing and have to plan methodically where to place my feet on

ABOVE • The husband-and-wife team of Emiliano and Danielle Del Bueno.
46 AVIATION CLASSICS

BELOW • 46 Aviation Classics perform what they call "the original style of wingwalking."
PHILIPPE REY VIA 46 AVIATION CLASSICS

46 AIRSHOWS OF THE WORLD 2025 WWW.KEY.AERO

the ribs so as not to damage the wing. The propwash and the wind are strong, so you have to be prepared for a fight – all the while smiling, waving to the crowd and maintaining elegance and poise."

What modifications have been made to the Stearman for wingwalking?
"The aircraft has a larger engine (450hp) than the standard 220hp Stearman. It has four ailerons, instead of the standard two, improving the aircraft's roll rate and agility. It has an inverted fuel and oil system allowing us to do an inverted pass. We have an environmentally friendly smoke system and a certified wingwalking rig.

What do you do during your show?
"I start off inside the cockpit and climb up to the top wing and attach myself to the rig. I do this in front of the crowd so they can see me make this transition. We have a few passes where I perform an aerobic/dance style routine as the plane performs level passes and stall turns. We fly an inverted pass and I then unstrap from the rig and lie across the leading edge.

"Next, I climb down and stand in front of the pilot's cockpit on one leg and perform the ballet pose named the Arabesque. On the next pass you'll see me climb from the cockpit as I walk out to the javelin [halfway between the wings].

ABOVE • *Danielle Del Bueno positions on the javelin between the wings.* EMILIANO DEL BUENO

RIGHT • *Emiliano Del Bueno is 46 Aviation Classics CEO and Swiss Unlimited Aerobatic Champion.* 46 AVIATION CLASSICS

I'm there for a loop and a roll, I then walk out even further to the far edges of the wing and wave to the crowd. We then perform our most exciting and most popular move where I hang upside down with my feet wrapped around the wing struts. It's the best part of the show! For the final pass, I sit on the lower wing, waving goodbye to the crowd, as the aeroplane flies in knife-edge.

"Emiliano uses the aeroplane to exhibit my wingwalking expertise and flies according to my needs and routine criteria. He carefully manages the aircraft's energy and makes regular adjustments due to my movements constantly altering the aircraft's centre of gravity.

"Emiliano complements the show by blending it with his intense, accomplished aerobatic training, looping, rolling and diving through the sky. We fly up to 125 knots, between 100ft-1,000ft depending on the manoeuvre, G forces ranging between -1 to 3G."

What is the difference between wingwalking and wingriding?
"Wingwalking is literally walking on and in between the wings and wingriding is when you are leaning against and strapped into the wingwalking rig/trapeze structure. During the inverted pass I am strapped into the rig due to the negative G, but for most of the show I like to change positions on the aircraft."

What safety steps do you take?
"On the top wing I have a certified wing-rack with a five-point harness which is secured with a second locking system called a locking pin. This secondary action prevents the harness being accidentally knocked open. For the entire duration of the display I have a harness around my waist and I am connected to the plane with short safety lines (less than a metre in length). I'm never free or loose on the aeroplane, I'm always attached. Emiliano is extremely experienced with flying taildraggers and aerobatics. He is also a Display Authorisation Examiner and is the Swiss Aerobatic Champion in the unlimited category, so I am in safe hands.

"The aeroplane is very well maintained and is certified and has been modified to accommodate for wingwalking. Our sequence has been thoughtfully planned out and considered, and every time we fly we discuss together the weather, wind direction and then we do a 'walk through' on the ground."

Where can we see you perform?
"We mostly perform in Italy, France and Switzerland. We have also performed in Greece, Spain, Belgium, Turkey, Czech Republic, Hungary, Denmark and the UK. We will update our website with our calendar and keep you posted on social media closer to summer." [The team is also announced for Airbourne in the UK.]

"We look forward to meeting you and seeing you at airshows. Please do wave to me when we are performing as I can see the waves from the sky and do come and say hello on the ground too, it's always nice to meet others passionate about aviation."
Website: www.46aviation.com/wingwalking ●

NORTH AMERICA

LEFT • *The USAF F-22 Raptor Demo Team is scheduled to perform at 23 airshows across North America in 2025.*
LANCE CPL SEFERINO GAMEZ/ US MARINE CORPS

LEFT • *A USAF Rockwell B-1B Lancer from the 419th Flight Test Squadron out of Edwards Air Force Base conducted a flyover of Huntington Beach, California, during the 2024 Pacific Airshow.*
RICHARD GONZALES/ US AIR FORCE

The team's website says: "There is nothing like experiencing a Thunderbirds performance in person. Watch powerful fighter jets elegantly manoeuvre in the sky with only a few feet separating each wingtip. It's a multisensory experience that will leave you impressed and inspired."

The Blue Angels are the US Navy Flight Demonstration Squadron with six Boeing F/A-18E/F Super Hornets at NAS Pensacola in Florida. The team's website says: "Around the country, the team serves as ambassadors of goodwill by bringing naval aviation to men, women and children across America. The precision flight demonstrations showcase the professionalism, excellence and teamwork found in all Navy and Marine Corps units, as well as provide the thrill and magic of flight to people each year."

Along with the Thunderbirds and the Blue Angels, the US military has several parachute display teams: the US Army Golden Knights, the USAF Wings of Blue, the US Navy Leap Frogs and the US Special Operations Command Para-Commandos.

Canada's contribution to North American airshows in 2025 is led each spring, in which the civilian/ACC demo team pilots train together and earn their certifications for the year's displays. There are 50-70 Heritage Flight demonstrations each year at events ranging from open houses/airshows to sporting events, parades and funerals. As the Davis-Monthan training flights in March 2025 showed, the formations vary in the composition of modern/historic aircraft. As Air Combat Command explained in its latest Demo Teams/Heritage Flight support manual for event organisers: "The heritage flights are usually scheduled as a package for airshows and open houses where an ACC single-ship demo team is scheduled to perform. The HFF is contracted to perform less shows than the demo teams are authorised to support, so not all shows will receive a heritage flight."

The US Navy Legacy Flight, operated by the Navy Legacy Flight Foundation, is the naval equivalent to the USAF Heritage Flight, in which the US Navy demo teams perform in close formation with historic aeroplanes flown by experienced civil pilots to honour US naval aviation/aviators then and now. The Legacy Flight has various historic naval aeroplanes at its disposal: Douglas A-1/AD-4 Skyraiders, Douglas A-4B/TA-4J Skyhawks, Chance Vought F4-U/Goodyear FG-1D Corsairs, North American T-2 Buckeyes, Grumman FM-2 Wildcats, F6F Hellcats and F8F Bearcats. Its programme involves these aircraft flying predominantly with the US Navy West/East Coast Super Hornet Demo Teams, which, as noted earlier, are from VFA-122 'Flying Eagles at NAS Lemoore and VFA-106 'Gladiators' at NAS Norfolk respectively. The F-35C has also joined the Legacy Flight programme.

Impressed and inspired

Along with the solo demo teams and the heritage/legacy flights, the modern US military contribution to airshows also includes the two air force and navy jet demonstration teams.

The Thunderbirds is the USAF Air Demonstration Squadron with six Lockheed Martin F-16C/D Fighting Falcon Block 52s, based at Nellis AFB northeast of Las Vegas, Nevada.

by the Royal Canadian Air Force Snowbirds (formally, 431 Demonstration Squadron) at 15 Air Base Moose Jaw, Saskatchewan, with its Canadair CT-114 Tutors, and the Canadian Forces Parachute Team, the SkyHawks.

The RCAF has stood down its CF-18 Hornet Demonstration Team for 2025. The RCAF will instead present a small number of non-aerobatic CF-18 tactical demonstrations from squadrons at CFB Cold Lake, Alberta, and CFB Bagotville, Québec, using aircraft in a standard operational grey paint scheme (the Canadians typically paint the CF-18 Demo Team aircraft in a colourful special livery each year). The format, the RCAF said, "will enable the RCAF to focus its resources as it modernises the fighter force [with F-35s], enhances its readiness to support ongoing domestic and international operations, and continues to carry out necessary training for experienced and new fighter pilots and technicians."

Coast to coast

An allocation of modern US military assets is a big deal for airshow organisers, so there's always anticipation for the International Council of Air Shows Convention in Las Vegas in December each year, where the calendars for the demo teams for the following year are announced.

Space constraints preclude listing appearances by all the North American military demo teams mentioned above. However, they are appearing at an extensive list of venues from coast to coast. Many of the major demo teams are as busy as ever in 2025 – the USAF Thunderbirds are scheduled for 32 airshows, while the F-35A Demo Team and F-22 Demo Team are each down for 23 events. The Blue Angels are scheduled for 34 airshows and the Snowbirds for 23.

Operational commitments mean some other demo teams only perform at a relatively small number of airshows each year. In 2025, the US Navy F-35C is scheduled for only eight airshows and the West Coast F/A-18E/F Rhino Demo Team for just six.

Some events receive multiple major demo team allocations in a

RIGHT • *B-29 Superfortresses* FIFI *and* Doc *in formation at EAA AirVenture 2024. The bombers will fly together again at Oshkosh in July 2025.* DYLAN PHELPS/ CENTERLINE IMAGES VIA EXPERIMENTAL AIRCRAFT ASSOCIATION

BELOW • *US Marine Corps F/A-18 Hornets assigned to 3rd Marine Aircraft Wing, I Marine Expeditionary Force, during the Marine Air-Ground Task Force demonstration of the 2024 MCAS Miramar Airshow in San Diego.* LANCE CPL SEFERINO GAMEZ/ US MARINE CORPS

NORTH AMERICA

ABOVE • *North American P-51 Mustangs at Oshkosh in 2024.* LAURIE GOOSSENS/EXPERIMENTAL AIRCRAFT ASSOCIATION

LEFT • *North America has numerous solo aerobatic pilots, such as Skip Stewart flying a customised Pitts S-2S called* Prometheus. GARY DANIELS/EXPERIMENTAL AIRCRAFT ASSOCIATION

single year. The Colombus Airshow at Rickenbacker International Airport in Colombus, Ohio, for example, will in 2025 host the USAF F-16 Viper Demo Team, a USAF Heritage Flight between the F-16 and a P-51 Mustang, the US Navy F-35C Demo Team and the Blue Angels. Herb Gillen, president of Herb Gillen Airshows, which organises the event, noted: "Rarely does the US Navy allow the F-35C to perform at the same show as the Blue Angels."

Other North American shows where multiple demo teams will be in attendance include the Boeing Seafair Airshow (Blue Angels, USMC F-35B, USAF F-35A and C-17).

Some North American airshows benefit from appearances by other units thanks to home-based units. For example, the US Marine Corps Air Station Miramar Airshow in San Diego, California, presents an annual Marine Air-Ground Task Force Demonstration, showcasing close air support, armour, artillery and infantry. Marine Corps F/A-18 Hornets fly over a wall of fire from a simulated air strike.

ABOVE • *Tora! Tora! Tora!* is the Commemorative Air Force's recreation of the Japanese attack on Pearl Harbor. MASTER SGT PATRICK EVENSON/US AIR NATIONAL GUARD

BELOW • Oshkosh 2025 will mark the centennial year of aircraft company Travel Air. SAM SASIN/ EXPERIMENTAL AIRCRAFT ASSOCIATION

The Experimental Aircraft Association's AirVenture Oshkosh at Wittman Regional Airport received a large contribution from the Wisconsin Air National Guard in 2024.

The US Air Force 115th Fighter Wing with F-35As simulated strafing and precision airstrikes, US Army 1st Battalion, 147th Aviation Regiment Sikorsky UH-60 Black Hawk helicopters delivered squads of infantry soldiers and simulated battlefield casualty evacuation, and a USAF 128th Air Refueling Wing Boeing KC-135R Stratotanker flew past with F-35As in mock air-to-air refuelling.

A Boeing B-1B Lancer from the 419th Flight Test Squadron flew across California from Edwards AFB to conduct a flyover of the 2024 Pacific Airshow at Huntington Beach. A KC-135R is scheduled for a flyover at the 2025 Colombus Air Show.

Aerobatics and barnstormers

North American shows are far more than US military aircraft thanks to the huge population of civilian performers, unrivalled in any other nation, that are involved in airshows across the continent.

There are formation aerobatics with classic aeroplanes from the Titan Aerobatic Team (four North American AT-6 Texans, the ex-AeroShell team), the Northern Stars Aeroteam in Canada (three Pitts Specials) and the NextGen Eagles Aerobatic Team (two Christen Eagle biplanes, the only team worldwide flying the type). The Atlanta, Georgia-based Full Throttle Formation Team is one of the largest display teams worldwide, flying a dozen Van's RV homebuilt aircraft. Undaunted Airshows is another RV team, using an RV-7 and an RV-8.

North America has numerous solo aerobatic pilots, such as Skip Stewart (flying a customised Pitts S-2S called *Prometheus*), Michael Goulian (Extra EA330SC), Kirby Chambliss (Zivko Edge 540), RJ Gritter (Bellanca Decathlon) and Brad Wursten (MXS).

Several acts uphold the decades-long tradition of barnstorming at North American airshows. There are wingwalking displays by Carol Pilon and Wingwalker Sam (both performed on a Boeing Stearman), while Jarrod Lindemann displays the sole flying Jet Waco (N32KP), a 1929 biplane equipped with a jet engine.

Erik Edgren performs comedy, dead-stick, power-on and night aerobatics in his 'T-Clips', a clipped-wing Taylor Monoplane. Other quirky acts include Kyle Fowler's bright yellow LongEz, and the Mini Jet, a highly modified kit-built aircraft with a 258lb-thrust PBS TJ-100 jet engine, giving the aircraft a 300mph top speed.

Wartime metal

As noted, in the US some civil-owned ex-military jets perform with the US Navy Legacy Flight, and there are other civil jet displays (see p.66), but it is piston-engined aircraft that really provide the history at North American airshows.

Two North American P-51 Mustang aerobatic teams put together examples of the classic fighter in close formation: The Horsemen Flight Team (Jim Beasley, Ed Shipley, Steve Hinton) and the Jack Aces Formation Aerobatic Team (Louis Horschel, Ariel Luedi, Marco Rusconi).

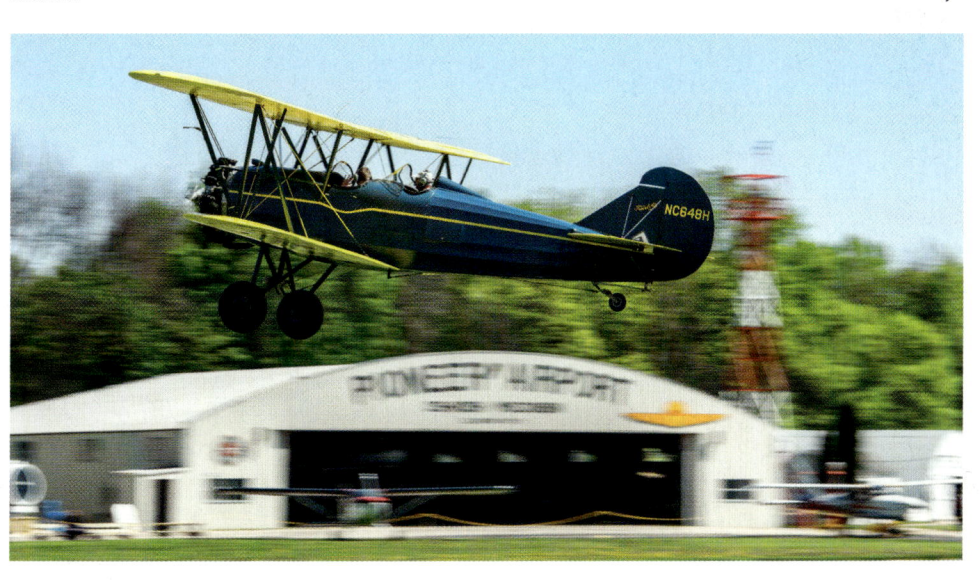

North America Airshows

May 2025

02-04	**Monroe Regional Airport, Louisiana** Red, White and Blue Airshow	www.redwhiteandblueairshow.com
02-04	**Fort Lauderdale, Florida** AirDotShow	www.fortlauderdaleairshow.com
03-04	**Seymour Johnson AFB, North Carolina** Wings Over Wayne Air Space and Technology Expo	www.wingsoverwayneairshow.com
09-10	**NAS Corpus Christi, Texas** Wings Over South Texas	www.wingsoversouthtexas.com
10-11	**Toledo Express Airport, Ohio** Toledo Air Show	www.toledoairshow.com
16-17	**Texas Regional Airport, Temple** Central Texas Airfest	www.flytemple.com/draughon-miller-central-texas-regional-airport/temple-airshow
16-17	**Illinois Valley Regional Airport, Peru, Illinois** TBM Avenger Gathering & Salute to Veterans	www.tbmreunion.org
17-18	**JB McGuire-Dix-Lakehurst, New Jersey** Power in the Pines Open House & Air Show
17-18	**Dalhart Municipal Airport, Texas** Thunder Over Dalhart	www.thunderoverdalhart.com
17-18	**Hillsboro Airport, Oregon** Oregon International Air Show	www. oregonairshow.com
17-18	**Brunswick Golden Isles Airport, Georgia** The Golden Isles Airshow	www.goldenislesairshow.com
21-23	**Annapolis, Maryland** US Naval Academy Air Show/Graduation Flyover
24-25	**Wantagh, New York** Bethpage Air Show at Jones Beach Park	www.bethpageairshow.com
24-25	**Miami Beach, Florida** Miami Beach Air & Sea Show 2025	www.usasalute.com
24-25	**Harrisburg International Airport, Pennsylvania** AirDotShow	www.air.show/centralpa
29	**USAF Academy, Colorado** US Air Force Academy Graduation
31-Jun 1	**Albuquerque/Kirtland AFB, New Mexico** Kirtland Air and Space Fiesta	www.kirtland.af.mil

June 2025

04	**North Bay, Ontario, Canada** Armed Forces Day
06-08	**Barrie, Ontario, Canada** Barrie Airshow Weekend	www.barrrie.ca
07-08	**Beale AFB, California** Open House	www.beale.af.mil
07-08	**Smyrna Airport, Tennessee** The Great Tennessee Air Show	www.greattennesseeairshow.com
13-15	**West Milford, New Jersey** NJ Air Show	www.njairshow.com
14	**Virginia Beach, Virginia** Flying Proms Symphonic Airshow	www.militaryaviationmuseum.org
14-15	**Minot AFB, North Dakota** Northern Neighbors Day Air & Space Show	www.minot.af.mil
14-15	**Ocean City, Maryland** Air Dot Show Ocean City	www.air.show/oceancity
14-15	**Olympia Regional Airport, Washington** Olympia Airshow	www.olympiaairshow.com
20-21	**Moses Lake Airport, Washington** Moses Lake Air Show	www.moseslakeairshow.com
21-22	**Dayton International Airport, Ohio** Dayton Air Show	www.daytonairshow.com
21-22	**Willow Run Airport, Ypsilanti, Michigan** Thunder Over Michigan Air Show	www.thunderovermichigan.org
28-29	**Chippewa Valley Regional Airport**
	Eau Claire, Wisconsin Chippewa Valley Air Show	www.chippewavalleyairshow.com
28-29	**Summerside Airport, Prince Edward Island, Nova Scotia, Canada** Air Show Atlantic	www.airshowatlantic.ca
28-29	**Tinker AFB, Oklahoma** Tinker Air Show	www.tinker.af.mil
28-29	**Traverse City, Michigan** National Cherry Festival Air Show	www.cherryfestival.org
28-29	**Wausau Downtown Airport, Wisconsin** Wings Over Wausau	www.wausauevents.org/events/wings-over-wausau

July 2025

02-06	**Battle Creek Executive Airport, Michigan** Battle Creek Field of Flight Air Show & Balloon Festival	www.fieldofflight.com
04	**Athens Municipal Airport, Texas** Thunder Over East Texas Air Show	www.thunderovereasttexas.com
05	**Cedar Creek Lake, Mabank, Texas** Thunder Over Cedar Creek Lake Air Show	www.ccveteransfoundation.org/thunder-over-cedar-creek-lake-airshow
05-06	**Canal Park, Duluth, Minnesota** Duluth Airshow	www.duluthairshow.com
11-13	**Bremerton National Airport, Washington** Bremerton Airshow	www.bremertonairshow.com
12-13	**Cocoa Beach, Florida** Air Dot Show Cocoa Beach	www.air.show/cocoabeach
12-13	**Fort Wayne ANG Base, Indiana** Fort Wayne Air Show	www.fwairshow.com
12-13	**Geneseo Airport, New York** Geneseo Airshow	www.nationalwarplanemuseum.com
12-13	**Pensacola Beach, Florida** Pensacola Beach Air Show	www.visitpensacola.com
18-20	**Southern Wisconsin Regional Airport, Janesville** Pistons and Props	www.pistonsprops.com
19-20	**Kingsley Field, Oregon** Sentry Eagle 2025 and Open House	www.173fw.ang.af.mil
19-20	**Boundary Bay Airport, Vancouver, Canada** Boundary Bay Airshow	www.czbb.com
19-20	**Milwaukee, Wichita:** Milwaukee Air & Water Show	www.mkeairwatershow.com
21-27	**Wittman Regional Airport, Oshkosh, Wisconsin** EAA AirVenture	www.eaa.org/airventure
25-27	**Kennewick/Pasco, Wichita** Tri-City Water Follies Air Show	www.waterfollies.com

August 2025

02-03	**Seattle, Wichita** Boeing Seafair Airshow	www.seafair.org/seafair-weekend-festival/air-show

North America Airshows (contd.)

02-03	**Fort St John, British Colombia, Canada**	Fort St John International Air Show | www.fsjairshow.com
08-10	**Abbotsford International Airport, British Colombia, Canada**	Abbotsford International Airshow | www.abbotsfordairshow.com
09-10	**MCAS Kaneohe Bay, Hawaii**	Marine Corps Base Hawaii Air Show | www.kaneohebayairshow.com
09-10	**Marquette Park, Gary, Indiana**	Gary Air Show Weekend | www.southshorecva.com/air-show
16-17	**Akron Fulton Airport, Ohio**	Props and Pistons Festival | www.flyohio.org
16-17	**Camarillo Airport, California**	Wings Over Camarillo | www.wingsovercamarillo.com
16-17	**Chicago, Illinois**	Chicago Air & Water Show | www.choosechicago.com
16-17	**Magic Valley Regional Airport, Twin Falls, Idaho**	Magic Valley Airshow | www.magicvalleyairshow.com
16-17	**Independence State Airport, Oregon**	Wings Over Willamette Fly-in & STOL WARS 2025 | www.wow-flyin.com
21-23	**Madras Municipal Airport, Oregon**	Airshow of the Cascades | www.cascadeairshow.com
23-24	**Davenport Municipal Airport, Iowa**	Quad City Air Show | www.quadcityairshow.com
23-24	**Orange County Airport, New York**	Air Dot Show | www.air.show/newyork
23-24	**Palmer Airport, Latrobe, Philadelphia**	Westmoreland County Air Show | www. www.westmorelandcountyairshow.com
23-24	**Rickenbacker International Airport, Colombus, Ohio**	Colombus Airshow | www.colombusairshow.com
23-24	**Villeneuve Airport, Edmonton, Alberta, Canada**	Alberta International Airshow | www.villeaero.com/airshow
30-Sept 1	**Batavia Airport, New York**	Wings Over Batavia Airshow | www.wingsoverbatavia.com
30-Sept 1	**Branson Airport, Missouri**	Branson Wings of Pride Airshow | www.bransonwingsofpride.com
30-Sept 1	**Burke Lakefront Airport, Cleveland, Ohio**	Cleveland National Air Show | www.clevelandairshow.com
30-Sept 1	**Toronto, Ontario, Canada**	Canadian International Airshow | www.cias.org

September 2025

05-07	**London International Airport, Ontario, Canada**	Airshow London | www.airshowlondon.com
05-07	**Mirabel International AeroCity, Québec, Canada**	Volaria Airshow | www.volaria.ca
06-07	**Laurinburg-Maxton Airport, North Carolina**	Sky High Aerospace Expo and Fly-In | www.skyhighexpo.com
06-07	**Midland International Air and Space Port, Texas**	CAF High Sky Wing AIRSHO | www.airsho.org
06-07	**Portsmouth International Airport, New Hampshire**	Thunder Over New Hampshire Air Show | www.thunderovernewhampshire.com
06-07	**Waukegan Regional Airport, Illinois**	Northern Illinois Airshow Wings Over Waukegab | www.northernillinoisairshow.com
10-14	**Roswell Air Center, New Mexico**	National Championship Air Races and Airshow | www.airrace.org
12-14	**Gatineau-Ottawa Executive Airport, Canada**	Aero Gatineau Ottawa | www.erogatineauottawa.com
12-14	**JB Andrews, Maryland**	JB Andrews Air Show www.jba.af.mil
13-14	**Greater Binghamton Airport, New York**	Greater Binghamton Air Show | www.binghamtonairshow.com
13-14	**Pryor Field Airport, Alabama**	North Alabama Airfest | www.flydcu.com/north-alabama-airfest
20-21	**NAS Oceana, Virginia**	NAS Oceana Air Show | www.oceanaairshow.com
20-21	**Northern Colorado International Airport**	The Great Colorado Air Show | www.greatcoloradoairshow.com
26-28	**MCAS Miramar, San Diego, California**	MCAS Miramar Air Show | www.miramarairshow.com
26-28	**McMinnville Airport, Oregon**	Oregon International Air Show | www. oregonairshow.com
27	**Spanish Fork, Utah**	Wings and Wheels | www.spanishfork.gov/airshow
27-28	**Pueblo Memorial Airport, Colorado**	Pueblo Wings of Pride Airshow | www.pueblowingsofpride.com

October 2025

03-05	**Salinas Airport, California**	California International Airshow | www.salinasairshow.com
04-05	**Huntington Beach, California**	Pacific Airshow | www.pacificairshowusa.com
04-05	**Tyler Pounds Airport, Texas**	Rose City Airfest | www.rosecityairfest.com
10-12	**San Francisco, California**	Fleet Week | www.fleetweeksf.org/air-show
11	**Apple Valley Airport, California**	Apple Valley Airshow | www.applevalleyairshow.com
11	**Culpeper Regional Airport, Virginia**	Culpeper Air Fest | www.culpeperairfest.com
11-12	**Falcon Field, Georgia:**	Air Dot Show Atlanta | www.airshowatlanta.com
11-12	**Hammond Northshore Regional Airport, Louisiana**	Hammond Northshore Regional Airshow | www.hammondairshow.com
18-19	**Biggs Army Airfield, El Paso, Texas**	Amigo Airshow | www.amigoairsho.com
18-19	**Ellington Airport, Houston, Texas**	Wings Over Houston Airshow | www.wingsoverhouston.com
18-19	**Russell Regional Airport, Rome, Georgia**	Wings Over North Georgia | www.wingsovernorthgeorgia.com
18-19	**Santa Maria Airport, California**	Central Coast Airfest | www.centralcoastairfest.com
24-26	**Jacksonville Beach, Florida**	Sea & Sky Airshow | www.specialevents.coj.net/special-events/sea-and-sky-airshow.aspx
25-26	**Orlando Sanford International Airport, Florida**	Air Dot Show Orlando | www.airandspaceshow.com

November 2025

01-02	**Keesler-Biloxi AFB, Massachusetts**	Thunder Over the Sound – Keesler/Biloxi Air & Space Show | www.thunderoverthesound.com
01-02	**Punta Gorda Airport, Florida**	Florida International Airshow | www.floridaairshow.com
01-02	**San Marcos Regional Airport, Texas**	San Marcos Airshow Wings & Warriors | www.sanmarcosairshow.com
07-08	**NAS Pensacola, Florida**	Blue Angels Homecoming Airshow | www.naspensacolaairshow.org
07-09	**Witham Field, Florida**	Stuart Airshow | www.stuartairshow.com

NORTH AMERICA

FIFI and Doc

Two other notable historic aeroplanes in the US are the only flying examples of the Boeing B-29 Superfortress bomber – *FIFI* (registered N529B, ex-US Army Air Force serial number 44-62070) and *Doc* (N69972, ex-44-69972). *FIFI* is owned and operated by the Commemorative Air Force in Dallas, Texas, and *Doc* by *Doc*'s Friends Inc., a Wichita, Kansas-based non-profit organisation.

August 2025 marks 80 years since the end of the World War Two, in which the B-29 played such a decisive part by dropping the atom bombs on Hiroshima and Nagasaki. This significant anniversary makes the schedule of air displays, ground events and passenger rides across the United States undertaken by *FIFI* and *Doc* especially poignant.

Both B-29s will be at AirVenture Oshkosh on July 21-27, 2025. The aircraft have made only around half-a-dozen joint public appearances since first flying together at Oshkosh in 2017. Three of those appearances have taken place at AirVenture, including in 2024.

Rick Larsen, EAA's vice president of communities and member programmes, who co-ordinates AirVenture features and attractions, said: "As AirVenture is the world's largest annual gathering of warbirds, bringing these two iconic aircraft together is another of those 'Only at Oshkosh' moments. These airplanes are big favourites wherever they appear separately, but together they will make the occasion even more unforgettable."

Each B-29 will spend time on EAA's Boeing Plaza, the centrepiece of the

The Commemorative Air Force (CAF) wings and squadrons across the United States constitute the world's largest flying collection of airworthy historic military aeroplanes. Its aircraft and pilots are a frequent sight at local and regional aviation events. The CAF collection comprised 181 aircraft (including those under restoration) at the time of writing in 2025, including 17 bombers, 11 fighters, 79 trainers, 44 liaison aircraft and 17 transports. The CAF also recreates the Japanese attack on Pearl Harbor that signalled the beginning of the American involvement in World War Two with its Tora! Tora! Tora! set-piece.

There are many other operators of vintage airframes who display World War Two aircraft at North American airshows, from private individuals (such as Vicky Benzing, who flies P-51D *Plum Crazy*) to organisations such as the Erickson Aircraft Collection in Oregon, which includes a B-17F Flying Fortress, B-25 Mitchell, P-51 Mustang, P-47D Thunderbolt, P-40E Kittyhawk, P-38 Lightning, Focke-Wulf Fw190, Lockheed P-2V7 Neptune and a Martin Mauler.

British classics also fly in North American skies. The Canadian Warplane Heritage Museum is home to Avro Lancaster FM213, C-GVRA, one of the only two airworthy Lancaster bombers. Four of the five examples of the de Havilland Mosquito currently airworthy are in North America: FB.26 KA114 with the Military Aviation Museum in Virginia Beach, the privately owned FB.VI PZ474, T.III TV959 with the Flying Heritage and Combat Armor Museum in Washington and B.35 VR796 with the KF Centre for Excellence in Kelowna, Canada.

ABOVE • *Undaunted Airshows, a Van's RV-7/RV-8 team from Shoreline, Washington, is one of the most prominent civil aerobatic teams in North America.* SENIOR AIRMAN JULIA LEBENS/US AIR FORCE

BELOW • *US Army 1st Battalion, 147th Aviation Regiment Sikorsky UH-60 Black Hawk helicopters perform a Wisconsin Air National Guard demo at Oshkosh 2024.* ANDREW ZABACK/EXPERIMENTAL AIRCRAFT ASSOCIATION

Oshkosh show. *FIFI* will be on display on July 21-23 and *Doc* on July 24-27. The two aircraft are scheduled to perform a formation flight at the beginning of the July 23 night airshow.

When it's not on display at Boeing Plaza, *Doc* will offer flight experiences on July 21-23 at Appleton International Airport, approximately 20 miles north of Oshkosh. *FIFI* will be in Appleton for flight experiences on July 24-27.

FIFI was acquired in the early 1970s by the Commemorative Air Force (then still the Confederate Air Force), when a group of CAF members found it at the US Navy Proving Ground at China Lake, California, where it was being used as a missile target. She was rescued and restored, then flew for more than 30 years until 2006, when the chief pilot decided to ground her pending a complete engine refit. After an extensive four-year restoration, which included installing four new custom-built hybrid engines, *FIFI* flew again in 2010.

Doc was built in 1944 and for many years was part of the 7th Radar Calibration Squadron at Griffiss AFB in upstate New York, a unit known as the 'Snow White and the Seven Dwarfs', hence the aircraft's name. It was retired in 1956 as the jet bomber age began. Like *FIFI*, it ended up as a target for US Navy training missions in China Lake, California, until 1998. A restoration group took possession of the aircraft from the US government and hauled it back in pieces to Wichita, Kansas, in 2000. After 16 years and more than 450,000 volunteer hours, *Doc* made its first flight after restoration in July 2016, 60 years after it had been retired.

Oshkosh to Huntington Beach

This year's Oshkosh is the 72nd annual edition of the EAA fly-in, convention and airshow, making it the longest-running airshow in the United States as well as the largest.

Oshkosh is unique in showcasing virtually every conceivable aspect of aviation. There's general aviation such as homebuilt airframes, ultralights and electric aircraft. There are vintage aircraft (this year's show will mark the centennial of Fairchild and Travel Air), World War Two fighters, transports and bombers, and ex-military jets. There are also airliners, business jets, turboprops, helicopters, modern military aircraft, aerobatics, barnstorming, flying with pyrotechnics, airships and spaceflight.

More aviation events take place in North America each year than in any other region worldwide, creating an almost dizzying array of airshows across the continent. There are the shows at major air bases including Marine Corps Air Station Miramar, Joint Base Andrews in Maryland and Naval Air Station Oceana in Virginia. Numerous events are also held at civil or city airports and airfields, including some well-established events such as the Commemorative Air Force's annual Airsho at Midland, Texas, celebrating its 35th year in 2025.

There are lakeside displays at the Chicago Air and Water Show and the Canadian International Air Show in Toronto, and seafront shows at the Pensacola Airshow in Florida and the Pacific Airshow Huntington Beach in Southern California. This year's Pacific Airshow is scheduled to include a display by a Luftwaffe Airbus A400M transport aircraft.

A perennial in the North American airshow scene in the autumn/fall is San Francisco Fleet Week, which sees displays in front of a stunning Bay backdrop including the Golden Gate Bridge. The National Championship Air Races is another fixture on the calendar at that time of year, which will feature a significant change this year: after almost 60 years at Reno Stead Airport in Nevada, the races move to a new venue at Roswell, New Mexico. ●

ABOVE • *Spectators get an up-close look at aircraft and helicopters, like this Boeing CH-47 Chinook from the US Army 1st Combat Aviation Brigade at North American airshows.* STAFF SGT FELIX MENA/US ARMY

RIGHT • *The USAF Heritage Flight brings together past and present combat aircraft, as seen here during training at Davis-Monthan Air Force Base, Arizona on March 1, 2025.* AIRMAN SAMANTHA MELECIO/US AIR FORCE

BELOW • *The US Army Golden Knights Parachute Team perform with Kirby Chambliss at the Amigo Airsho at Biggs Army Airfield, Fort Bliss, Texas in 2024.* STAFF SGT FELIX MENA/US ARMY

WWW.KEY.AERO AIRSHOWS OF THE WORLD 2025 57

WORLDWIDE

Worldwide

Airshows provide aerial entertainment and a platform for business all around the world

BELOW • *The UAE Air Force Fursan Al Emarat display during the 2023 Langkawi International Maritime and Aerospace Exhibition 2023 in Malaysia.*
ANNICE LY/GETTY IMAGES

Most airshows take place in North America and Europe, but large air displays happen worldwide. Early 2025 saw a couple of large shows in the Asia-Pacific region.

Aero India

Aero India is a biennial airshow and aviation exhibition at Air Force Station Yelahanka near Bengaluru in India, organised by the Defence Exhibition Organisation in the Department of Defence Production within the Indian Ministry of Defence. In 2025, it took place on February 10-14.

As the country's premier aerospace/defence exhibition, Aero India sees the Indian Air Force put on displays and flypasts of various types, from fighters and transports to helicopters and trainers. For international visitors, the show provides a rare opportunity to see all these types together.

In 2025, the display included a flypast of various elements. It started with an Akash (Antonov An-32), followed by three Dhwaj helicopters (Mil Mi-17s), three Hindustan Aeronautics Ltd (HAL) Tejas, three HAL Bhim light utility helicopters, three Indian Coast Guard Dornier 228s and an Antonov An-32 in formation with two Do 228s.

The flypast continued with four more Tejas, a formation of Indian Navy Boeing P-8I flanked by two MiG-29Ks and two BAE Systems Hawk Mk 132s and a Lockheed Martin C-130J with two Airbus C295s. There were then four Jaguars, an Embraer Netra (an airborne early warning/control-configured Embraer ERJ-145), a Rafale with two Sukhoi Su-30MKIs and finally three more Su-30MKIs.

As well as this flypast, Aero India 2025 included solo displays by Su-30MKI and Tejas jets. There was a display by the Dornier 228 testbed operated by HAL for India's Defense Research and Development Organization, used as a flying laboratory for advanced aerospace systems, sensors and technologies.

The Indian Air Force's Surya Kiran Aerobatic Team (SKAT), which flies Hawk Mk 132s, was part of the flying programme, as were several HAL trainers: the Hansa NG (ab-initio), HTT-40 (basic) and HJT-36 Sitara (intermediate jet).

For the static display, the Indian Air Force brought a C-130J, Dassault Rafale, Jaguar DARIN III (Display, Attack, Ranging and Inertial Navigation System, the latest avionics upgrade of the aircraft), a C-295 and a Netra. The Indian Coast Guard showed a Do 228, and the Indian Navy displayed a MiG-29K, Kamov KM-31, Sikorsky MH-60R and Sea King 42B/42Cs, while HAL presented a Tejas, HTT-40, HJT-36, a light utility helicopter and the Pranchand light combat helicopter.

Overseas participants in the static park at AERO India 2025 included US Air Force Lockheed Martin F-35A Lightning and F-16 Fighting Falcon, while Russia sent its fifth-generation fighter, the Sukhoi Su-57.

Avalon

Another major Asia-Pacific airshow early in 2025 was the Australian International Airshow at Avalon Airport southwest of Melbourne in the state of Victoria. The trade days were on March 25-28 and the public days on March 28-30. As with other industry events worldwide, the trade element of Avalon included a conference, symposia and presentations, an exhibition, formal networking, VIP/international delegations and pavilions, as well as static aircraft and flying displays.

In 2025, the Royal Australian Air Force (RAAF) contributed flying and static F-35A Lightnings, Boeing F/A-18F Super Hornets, Boeing P-8A Poseidons and Leonardo C-27J Spartans, plus a flying Lockheed Martin C-130J, Boeing C-17A Globemaster and an Airbus KC-30A tanker. RAAF aircraft on static included an E-7A Wedgetail, EA-18G Growler and MQ-25 Ghost Bat.

The Australian Defence Force Red Beret Parachute Team performed in the flying display, and the army showed a Boeing CH-47 Chinook, Sikorsky UH-60M Black Hawk and Integrator drone in the static display. The Royal Australian Navy sent a Sikorsky MH-60R Romeo for the flying and static displays and an Airbus Helicopters EC135 for the static.

The public airshow at Avalon included performances by the Roulettes, the RAAF Aerobatic Team with Pilatus PC-21s. There were also several historic aircraft from 100 Squadron, the RAAF heritage unit that operates a diverse fleet of ex-RAAF types from two locations, RAAF Base Point Cook near Melbourne and Temora Aviation Museum in New South Wales.

No 100 Squadron was reformed in January 2021 to coincide with the RAAF's centenary. Its fleet includes a couple of rare historic gems: English Electric Canberra

AIRSHOWS OF THE WORLD 2025 59

WORLDWIDE

TT18 VH-ZSQ and Gloster Meteor F.8 VH-MBX, now the only flying examples of these classic British jets. The No 100 fleet also includes a de Havilland DH115 Vampire VH-VAM and CA-27 Sabre VH-IPN, although, as the Royal Australian Air Force website notes, the Sabre is currently not flying owing to technical support issues with the legacy ejection seats.

Other aircraft in the No 100 Squadron fleet include CA-13 Boomerang VH-MHR, Cessna A-37B Dragonfly VH-XVA and two of only three airworthy Supermarine Spitfires in Australia: Mk VIII VH-HET and Mk XVI VH-XVI. The 100 Squadron historic aircraft on show at Avalon 2025 comprised the Spitfire Mk VIII, CAC CA-18 Mustang (VH-SVU), PAC CT/4A trainer (VH-NZP) and a CA-25 Winjeel (VH-FTS).

The international military presence at Avalon 2025 included the USAF Lockheed Martin F-22 Raptor Demonstration Team, a C-17A and the Pacific Air Forces F-16 Demonstration Team. The static featured a US Army AH-64E Apache, Luftwaffe Airbus A400M, Royal New Zealand Air Force Boeing 757-2K2 and C-130J, a Republic of Singapore Air Force CH-47 and a Papua New Guinea Defence Force P-750.

ABOVE • *Royal Australian Air Force Boeing F/A-18F Hornets take off at Avalon in 2019.* CPL JESSICA DE ROUW/ROYAL AUSTRALIAN AIR FORCE

LEFT • *A Royal Australian Air Force Boeing F/A-18F Super Hornet taxies in after a display at Avalon in 2023.* LACW ANNIKA SMIT/ROYAL AUSTRALIAN AIR FORCE

RIGHT • *Royal Australian Air Force Lockheed Martin F-35A Lightning.* AB SUSAN MOSSOP/ROYAL AUSTRALIAN AIR FORCE

RIGHT • *A No. 100 Squadron Supermarine Spitfire MK VIII taxis at the Australian International Airshow 2025.* LAC CAMPBELL LATCH/ROYAL AUSTRALIAN AIRFORCE

BELOW • *The No.100 Squadron CA-13 Boomerang takes off at Temora Aerodrome, New South Wales.* CPL KYLIE GIBSON/ROYAL AUSTRALIAN AIR FORCE

As well as the trade and public airshows, static displays and exhibitions, Avalon featured an evening airshow incorporating pyrotechnic displays. (See p.80 for more on pyro airshows.) In 2025, the Friday Night Alight display included sunset displays by the F-16, F-22, Roulettes, a parachute drop with pyros by Rod Benson, a Cessna 185 with pyros displayed by Paul Bennet, flare-drops by a Royal Australian Navy 808 Squadron MH-60R and Royal Australian Air Force 37 Squadron C-130J, and the show's traditional Wall of Fire finale.

Gold Coast

An upcoming major airshow in Australia in 2025 will be Pacific Airshow Gold Coast in Queensland on August 15-17, 2025.

This event is put on by the same organisers who run the Pacific Airshow at Huntington Beach in Southern California each October. The organisers describe the Australian version of the event as "the largest airshow to ever take place in Australia, with more than 250,000 spectators."

Pacific Airshow says the event is not just another airshow but "a global spectacle-scale celebration of mateship, family, friends and awe-inspiring feats of aviation meshed with the enticing thrill of sports, entertainment, art and technology."

At the time of writing, there was no information about the air displays planned for 2025, but the previous event included the RAAF Roulettes, F-35A Lightning and F/A-18F Super Hornet, and the Australian Defence Force Red Berets Parachute Team. There was a substantial international involvement in Gold Coast 2024, with the US Air Force F-22 Raptor Demo Team, plus C-17 Globemaster III and KC-135R Stratotanker, a US

WWW.KEY.AERO AIRSHOWS OF THE WORLD 2025 61

WORLDWIDE

World Airshows

May 2025
- 04 — **MCAS Iwakuni, Japan** MCAS Iwakuni Airshow Friendship Day | www.iwakuniairshow.com
- 09-10 — **Nelspruit Airport, Nelspruit, South Africa** Lowveld Air Show | www.lowveldairshow.co.za
- 10-11 — **Osan AB, South Korea** Osan Air Power Day 2025 | www.osan.af.mil
- 17-18 — **Yokota AB, Japan** Japanese-American Friendship Festival | www.yokota.af.mil
- 20-24 — **Langkawi International Airport, Malaysia** LIMA 25 Langkawi International Maritime and Aerospace Exhibition | www.lima2025.com
- 25 — **JASDF Miho, Japan** JASDF Open House – Miho Air Base Air Show | www.mod.go.jp

June 2025
- 01 — **JGSDF Camp Kamifurano, Hokkaido, Japan** 70th Anniversary Kamifurano Garrison
- 08 — **JASDF Hofu, Japan** JASDF Open House – Hofu Air Show | www.mod.go.jp
- 25-27 — **Wonderboom Airport, Pretoria, South Africa** AERO South Africa

August 2025
- 15-17 — **Gold Coast, Queensland, Australia** Pacific Airshow Gold Coast | www.pacificairshowaus.com
- 31 — **JASDF Matsushima, Japan** JASDF Open House - Matsushima Air Show | www.mod.go.jp

September 2025
- 20 — **Temora Airport, Australia** Temora Aviation Museum September Showcase | www.aviationmuseum.com.au/events
- 21 — **JASDF Misawa Air Base, Japan** JASDF Open House – Misawa Air Base Air Show | www.mod.go.jp
- 21 — **Tocumwal Airport, Australia** Tocumwal Airshow | www.tocumwalairshow.com.au

October 2025
- 18 — **Temora Airport, Australia** Temora Aviation Museum October Showcase | www.aviationmuseum.com.au/events
- 19 — **JASDF Gifu, Japan** JASDF Open House – Gifu Air Base Air Show | www.mod.go.jp
- 26 — **JASDF Hamamatsu, Japan** JASDF Open House – Air Fiesta Hamamatsu | www.mod.go.jp
- 29 – Nov 02 — **Seoul, South Korea (venue TBC)** Seoul International Aerospace & Defense Exhibition 2025 | www.seouladex.com

November 2025
- 03 — **JASDF Iruma, Japan** JASDF Open House – Iruma Air Show | www.mod.go.jp
- 17-21 — **Dubai World Central, UAE** Dubai Airshow 2025 | www.dubaiairshow.aero
- 30 — **JASDF Tsuiki, Japan** JASDF Open House – Tsuiki Air Festival | www.mod.go.jp

December 2025
- 02-04 — **Lagos Airport, Nigeria** Nigeria International Airshow | www.nigeriaairshow.ng

---

International Airshow in Malaysia is scheduled for May 20-24, 2025, and the next Dubai Airshow at Dubai World City will take place on November 17-21, 2025. According to the organisers of the latter: "Dubai Airshow 2025 is set to redefine the boundaries of aviation, space and defence. This year's event will not only celebrate cutting-edge advances, but also pioneer new pathways in sustainable aviation, inspiring the industry toward a more connected, innovative and eco-conscious future. Over five thrilling days, Dubai will become the centre stage for global leaders, showcasing the latest technologies, visionary aircraft and an electrifying flying display. By uniting the best minds and boldest innovators, Dubai Airshow 2025 marks a new era, driving the industry forward and strengthening the UAE's role as a leader in the aerospace revolution."

Trade airshows always feature the latest commercial aircraft in the flying/static displays. At the last Dubai event, in 2023, Airbus showed the A350-1000, A330-900neo (new engine option) and A320 P2F (passenger-to-freighter conversion), while Boeing presented a 777-9 – one of relatively few public appearances for the delayed latest version of the Triple Seven – and two 787-9 Dreamliners.

The United Arab Emirates' home carriers always send aircraft. In 2023, Emirates contributed an Airbus A380 and Boeing 777-300ER, flydubai sent a 737-8 and Etihad Airways had a 787-9. Saudia showed a 787-10 and an A320neo, while Qatar Airways sent an A350-1000 and 787-9. Various business jets also attended: a new Airbus ACJ TwoTwenty, Bombardier Challenger 3500 and Global 7500, Dassault Falcon 6X, Falcon 10X and Falcon 2000LXS, Embraer Praetor 600, Gulfstream G700

BELOW • *Japan Air Self-Defense Force events present rare opportunities to see current Japanese military aircraft, such as (left to right) a Fuji T-7, Mitsubishi F-2 and F-15J Eagle.* TOM JONES

and G500 and Pilatus PC-24. Qatar Airways Executive sent a Bombardier Global 7500 and Gulfstream G650ER, and there was a RoyalJet BBJ (Boeing Business Jet) 737-700.

A new feature for Dubai 2025 is a flying display of electric vertical take-off and landing (eVTOL) systems – aka air taxis – which have attracted billions of dollars in investment and numerous orders in recent years. According to the organisers: "Following the successful launch of the Advanced Air Mobility pavilion, the 2025 show will once again witness an exclusive showcase of future flight technologies. The event will also combine an exhibition area featuring revolutionary products, eVTOLs on the static and flying display and the return of the AAM conference programme addressing the way we travel, the regulations and infrastructure and how we incorporate AAM into our daily lives."

Fighters

Although participation details for Dubai will not be finalised until much closer to the event, a considerable military involvement is expected. The Dubai show in 2023 was notable for the first public air displays by the two latest-generation examples of the Boeing F-15 fighter: a Qatar Emiri Air Force F-15QA Ababil and an F-15EX Eagle II. Other military participants included an Embraer C-390 Millennium, the Brazilian manufacturer's new multi-mission aircraft, two Armée de l'Air et l'Espace (French Air and Space Force) Dassault Rafales and two examples of the Pakistan Aeronautical Complex/Chengdu Aircraft Corporation JF-17 Thunder fighter.

China's CATIC showed a pair of L-15 advanced jet trainers painted in the colours of the UAE Air Force Aerobatic Team, Fursan Al Emarat. It was announced during the show that this team would re-equip later in the 2020s, with the L-15 replacing their Aermacchi MB.339NAT (National Aerobatic Team) aircraft. Fursan Al Emarat performs at Dubai and joint flypasts have involved the team trailing behind an Emirates airliner – typically an A380 – streaming multicoloured smoke.

Looking further ahead, 2026 is due to see the next editions of Airshow China, the Singapore Airshow and the Bahrain International Airshow. ●

ABOVE • *Blue Impulse, the Japan Air Self-Defense Force aerobatic team.*
TOM JONES

BELOW • *The Black Eagles, the Republic of Korea Air Force aerobatic team, in Singapore in 2024.*
ROSLAN RAHMAN/AFP VIA GETTY IMAGES

JETS

Fast Jets

The spectacle of modern and historic jets is a key element of airshows

ABOVE • *The Harrierahs been a popular feature at airshows for decades. Here, a Spanish Navy EAV-8B+ performs at RIAT 2024.* NIGEL WATSON

The USAF F-22 Raptor is at the cutting edge of modern fighter aircraft design.

This highly sophisticated fifth-generation combat jet, according to the USAF, "cannot be matched by any known or projected fighter aircraft." Capable of both air-to-air and air-to-ground missions, the Raptor has advanced flight controls, supercruise (flying at supersonic speeds without afterburner), high manoeuvrability and integrated avionics.

The USAF F-22 Demonstration Team showcases the Raptor's speed, agility, technology, powerful engines and startling thrust vectoring capability. The demo is unlike any other modern fighter display – its sequence providing a blend of high-G turns, powerful climbs, tight manoeuvring at steep angles and startling, rapid changes of direction.

The 1st Fighter Wing at Langley Air Force Base, Virginia, is home to the Raptor Demo Team. It typically displays at around 20-25 airshows in North America each year, making appearances by the aircraft much anticipated by organisers and attendees of the events to which it is allocated.

The F-22 displayed at the Australian International Airshow at Avalon in March 2025 and has appeared at the Royal International Air Tattoo (RIAT) at RAF Fairford in the UK in 2010 and 2017, although generally the F-22 rarely performs overseas.

The American military offers other fast jet displays – there are US Air Force, US Navy and US Marine Corps F-35 Lightning II demos, the USAF F-16C Fighting Falcon and USN F/A-18E/F Super Hornet teams.

Hornets and Gripens

Two air forces have stood down fast jet displays for 2025: the Royal Canadian Air Force's CF-18 Hornet Demonstration Team and the Swiss Air Force's F/A-18C Hornet solo. Both air arms cited operational pressures for the decisions when they were announced late in 2024.

However, many other nations maintain fast jet displays. There's the RAF Eurofighter Typhoon FGR4 solo display, Czech Air Force Saab JAS39C Gripen, Royal Danish Air Force F-16AM (see p.86), French Air and Space Force Dassault Rafale and Finnish Air Force F-18C Hornet teams. The Hellenic Air Force displays the F-16C Block 52+ (aka the Zeus Demo Team). There's also the Hungarian Air Force JAS39C Gripen, Italian Air Force Eurofighter EF2000 Typhoon and Leonardo T-346A Master, Luftwaffe EF2000 and Tornado IDS, Polish Air Force F-16C, Spanish Air and Space Force EF2000 (locally designated C.16 Tifon) and EF-18M Hornet, Spanish Navy EAV-8B Harrier, Swedish Air Force JAS39C Gripen and Turkish Air Force F-16C (aka SoloTurk). For nations without a dedicated national display team, such as Czechia, Hungary and Sweden, a fast-jet solo is a flagship for the country overseas as well as representing the air force.

Most modern military fast jet displays showcase turning performance, roll rates and vertical manoeuvres, although there are differences between them due to how each nation chooses to present its routine. Recent fly-by-wire flight control system updates on Finnish/Spanish Hornets, for example, enable these air arms to perform striking manoeuvres at slow speeds and high angles of attack. The French Rafale display, by contrast, typically focuses on complex rolling sequences. Sweden's Gripen display concludes with a remarkable short-field landing, while Hungary's Gripen demo includes a 'dump and burn', where fuel vented from the tailfin is ignited by the afterburner.

Harrier and Tornado

There are some military fast jet displays/demos of an older vintage, such as the Spanish Navy with its McDonnell Douglas EAV-8B+ Harrier II aircraft from 9 Escuadrilla at Base Navale de Rota near Cadiz. Spain is the last nation to regularly display the Harrier, as neither the US Marine Corps nor the Italian Navy do so.

The EAV-8B+ routine follows the long tradition of Harrier displays, with high-speed passes showing the aircraft as a conventional fast jet, before a sequence of 'jetborne' flight – hovering, sideways and backwards flying – to show the thrust-vectoring performance of the aircraft's Rolls-Royce Pegasus engine. The Harrier's popularity remains undimmed judging by crowd reactions to recent EAV-8B+ displays at RIAT.

The Harrier is not the only veteran fast jet still in service that air forces display at airshows. The Finnish Air Force has a solo British Aerospace Hawk Mk66 display from its Air Force Academy at Rovaniemi, performed by an aircraft from its Midnight Hawks display team. In 2025, the Luftwaffe (German Air Force) has a Panavia Tornado IDS demo from TLG 33 (Fighter Bomber Wing 33) at Büchel Air Base near the city of Cochem

RIGHT • *The USAF F-22 Demonstration Team is provided by the 1st Fighter Wing at Langley Air Force Base.* GARY DANIELS/EXPERIMENTAL AIRCRAFT ASSOCIATION

ABOVE • *The Czech Air Force only has 14 Saab JAS 39 Gripens, but its solo display travels to various European countries each year.*
SHAUN SCHOFIELD

in Rhineland. A schedule released in March 2025 revealed the Tornado will appear at only two venues this year: the Antidotum Airshow Leszno in Poland and the Malta International Airshow.

Tornado displays are now very rare – Europe's only other Tornado operator, the Italian Air Force, no longer displays its PA200 Tornado. The Luftwaffe last displayed the Tornado more than 20 years ago and the type has only been seen at airshows on a limited basis since then, either on static display, flying past briefly at the biennial ILA Berlin Air Show or in an air-to-air refuelling demo with a Luftwaffe Airbus A400M Atlas as at RIAT 2023.

There is a revived enthusiasm for display flying in the Luftwaffe just now. As well as the Tornado and an Airbus A400M transporter, there are two EF2000 solo displays in 2025, one from TLG 31 at Nörvenich Air Base in North-Rhine Westphalia and one from TLG 74 at Neuburg Air Base in Bavaria.

According to information released by the Luftwaffe in March 2025, the TLG 31 Eurofighter will appear at the Paris Air Show, Kecskemet in Hungary, Bucharest International Air Show, Athens Flying Week and NATO Days at Ostrava in Czechia, as well as a domestic show at Bückeberg.

The TLG 74 display is scheduled for two domestic shows at Schleswig/Jagel and Siegerland, the Czech Air Force Open Day at Čáslav, the Antidotum Airshow Leszno and Radom International Airshow in Poland and the Roskilde Airshow in Denmark. Both EF2000 display pilots will perform at the Malta International Airshow.

Resources

Generating a fast jet display/demo is resource-intensive for air arms. It is not just about aircraft or pilots, but has to take into account budgets, squadron flying hours, engineering impacts and how training/rehearsals and attending events fit around a unit's primary taskings and training.

Air arms sometimes simply just don't have the capacity to put on a show, as per the Canadians and Swiss decisions for 2025. If they do, they might be highly selective about events, meaning they appear on a limited basis, as shown by the Luftwaffe Tornado/Eurofighter schedules in 2025.

Nevertheless, air arms try to do their best. The Czech Air Force, for example, has only 14 Saab JAS 39 Gripen fighters (12 single-seat JAS 39Cs and two twin-seat JAS 39Ds) assigned to its 211th Tactical Squadron at Čáslav, southeast of Prague. These fighters are busy – they provide quick reaction alert air defence not only for Czechia but for neighbouring Slovakia while that country builds its own new F-16 force, and they undertake NATO air policing deployments in the Baltic and Iceland. Even so, the Czechs sent their Gripen display to events in Austria, Belgium, Estonia, Slovakia, the UK and domestic airshows in 2024. The Sanicole Airshow in Belgium is on the 2025 agenda at the time of writing.

Classic jets

Current military aircraft are not the only fast jet displays. The Swedish Air Force Historic Flight displays various Saab fighters: an AJS 37 Viggen (SE-DXN), SK 37 Viggen (SE-DXO), J 35J Draken (SE-DXR), SK 35C Draken (SE-DXP), three J 32 Lansens (SE-RMD, SE-RME, SE-RMF), a J 29 Tunnan (SE-DXB), an SK 60/Saab 105 (SE-DXG) and a J 34 Hawker Hunter SE-DXM.

In the UK, aerobatics by swept-wing classic jets over land are prohibited. This ruling does not apply to seaside airshows, which has enabled the SwAFHF to perform aerobatic displays with its Draken, Tunnan and Viggen at several British coastal venues in recent years.

Norway is another Scandinavian country whose air force has a dedicated historic flight. The Norwegian Air Force Historical Squadron has a MiG-15UTI (N104CJ), two de Havilland Vampires (FB.52 LN-DHY and T.11 LN-DHZ) and a Canadair CT-133 Shooting Star (LN-DPS).

UK-based classic jets include the Strikemaster Display Team from North Wales Military Aviation Services at Hawarden, near Chester, and Jet Aviation's Jet Provost T5A (serial number XW324/G-BWSG). At North Weald in Essex, there's the Gnat Display Team and de Havilland Vampire T11 WZ507/G-VTII. An Aero L-29 Delfin (G-BYCT) owned by a company called G-BKOU/2 Ltd is due to perform at the 2025 Midlands Air Festival, marking the first display by the type at a British airshow in more than a decade.

Elsewhere in Europe, Mistral Warbirds in Avignon, France, operates F-86E Sabre F-AYSB (a Canadair-built, ex-Luftwaffe CL 13B Sabre Mk6 later used as a target tug). Other French historic jets include Armor Aéro Passion's MS760 Paris (F-AZLT) and Patrouille Tranchant, a team of Fouga CM170 Magisters. The Warsaw, Poland-based Fundacja Eksadra (Squadron Foundation) offers a MiG-15 (SP-MIG) and MiG-15UTI (SP-YNZ); it is currently restoring a MiG-17.

There are MiG-17s in the US, too, including the all-red MiG-17F NX117BR flown by Jason Somes of High Alpha Aviation, the aircraft formerly sponsored by Red Bull and displayed by the late Bill Reesman for many years. MiG-17F/MiG-17PFs equip the FighterJets Demo Team led by Randy Ball. Other civil jet displays in the US include the Patriots Jet Team of Aero L-39 Albatros and solo/duo Canadair T-33 Shooting Stars from Ace Maker Aviation LLC in California. ●

RIGHT • *MiG-17s in formation in the United States in 2024.*
NICK MOORE/EXPERIMENTAL AIRCRAFT ASSOCIATION

Midlands Air Festival

From fast jets to the flying circus, hot air balloons and helicopters

The Midlands Air Festival at Ragley Hall in Warwickshire is unique in the UK, combining an international air display, Europe's largest gathering of hot air balloons and Nightfire, a twilight show with pyrotechnic air displays, hot air balloons and fireworks.

Now in its seventh year, the Midlands Air Festival has quickly become a UK airshow success story. As well as the aviation, there are multiple family attractions and entertainments on the ground. The show takes place in the historic surroundings of the Ragley Hall Estate, the stately home of the Marquis of Hertford.

Classic airshow

Trevor Graham is a director of Slipstream Management, the company that conceived, designed, and entirely operates the Midlands Air Festival. He said the location is part of the charm: "It's a good viewing area. It's good for our balloons and the fast jets and the Red Arrows. It's very enclosed and intimate and we tend to get aircraft as close as we possibly can to the crowd legally. Our admittedly small runway is right in front of everybody, so they can see everything landing and taking off."

The event hosts a diverse range of aircraft – there are thunderous fast jets, classic warbirds, vintage aeroplanes, colourful display teams, barnstorming, high-energy aerobatics, radio-controlled models, hot air balloons and the dusk shows with pyrotechnics/lights. No other aviation event in the UK provides quite this much diversity.

RIGHT • *Midlands Air Festival at Ragley Hall is a classic British airshow.*
MIDLANDS AIR FESTIVAL

BELOW • *There will be early-morning hot air balloon launches, weather permitting.*
MIDLANDS AIR FESTIVAL

"We felt there was a market for a classic airshow, a classic air festival, with everything," Trevor said. "When we decided to run the show, we agonised over the name. We came up with the Midlands Air Festival because we wanted to put everything that we could possibly get flying into the show, so we could attract all sorts of people.

"One of the reasons I started [the show] was because I felt the scene was falling apart, there were no new shows. Me and my business partners had a conversation at a windswept balloon event, where we ended up with three balloons in the rain. We decided we should have a crack at putting on an air festival with our combined experiences."

Attracting people

Trevor has extensive grounding in air displays and balloon festivals going back more than 40 years through involvement at countless major events, including the Biggin Hill Air Fair, the Great Warbirds Air Display, Fighter Meet at North Weald and Flying Legends at Duxford. Over the years, he's worked as a commentator, creative producer, technical communications director, flying control committee member, licensed radio operator and flying display director. It was, he said, "a no-brainer" to combine an airshow with a bit of everything, along with hot air balloons and building on the night-glow events that have long been part of balloon festivals.

This approach has drawn in new attendees – according to the festival's research, 45% of visitors had never visited an airshow before: "Once you get them there, they become regulars. We attract lots of families with children – we like to think we're doing our own little bit in inspiring the next generation."

Time passing is one reason why Midlands Air Festival has adopted a distinctive 'variety show' approach, blending different aspects of aviation: "The thing we've got to remember is that we're losing the direct contact with World War Two. We went through a period of 'my dad flew in the war', and now we're into 'my grandad or great grandad flew in the war'. It's not quite so powerful as it was when you had a living relative and had that natural curiosity about their experiences."

Trevor thinks one reason why the now long-gone Great Warbirds Air Display and Fighter Meet (last held in 1994 and 1997 respectively) became so popular back in the 1980s was because there were still many people around who had

ABOVE • *Mistral Warbirds' F-86 Sabre.* PAUL JOHNSON

served during World War Two: "It used to be 'grandad's always talking about Spitfires, let's go and see a Spitfire'. You haven't got that at all now. So it's not such a shoo-in to lay on a great load of warbirds and expect everybody to come to the show."

The Midlands Air Festival's approach is "putting on the things the majority of people want to see: the Red Arrows, the Typhoons, the jets. Then, when we get them there, we'll show them the rarer warbirds and tell the history." This differs, he said, from "doing a show where you're going to get a lot of warbird enthusiasts but few non air display people. You'll never see 14 Spitfires at Midlands, but you'll always see one or two, and, to our audience, that's enough."

Red Bull helicopter

Even so, it's worth emphasising that aircraft prized by enthusiasts are still firmly on the agenda at Ragley Hall. The Commemorative Air Force Douglas R4D-6S *Ready 4 Duty* will visit the 2025 show during its European tour (see p70). The Red Bull Flying Bulls in Austria (see p94) will send the remarkable, aerobatic MBB Bölkow Bo 105C.

Frédéric Akary will bring his F-86 Sabre from his Mistral Warbirds stable in Avignon, France. Weather and operational reasons precluded a display by this aircraft at the 2024 show. An F-86 hasn't flown in Britain since the Golden Apple Trust-owned F-86A G-SABR, now N48178 with Heritage Air LLC in Oklahoma, left in 2014.

Team Niebergall, a SIAI-Marchetti SF260 duo from Germany who perform aerobatics with smoke, will be another UK airshow debutant. Trevor said: "I picked them up from YouTube. They were different, which is always a very good thing for us."

These overseas participants follow performances at the 2024 show by the Flying Bulls' Douglas DC-6B (OE-LDM) and B-25J Mitchell (N6123C) and the Swedish Air Force Historic Flight's Saab J 35J Draken SE-DXR.

A lot of planning is required to enable civil aircraft from overseas to display in the UK. Trevor explained: "We have to find an official display authorisation examiner (DAE) who can provide a DA for the type of aircraft that are coming over, and DAEs are in short supply. They have to either go over to the country of origin and see them fly – that's what we did with the Draken, our DAE went to the base in Sweden, reviewed them and gave them their DA – or we've got to get them here early to fly their sequence and the DAE will give them a UK authorisation."

The UK Civil Aviation Authority and European Union Aviation Safety Agency (EASA) had an agreement enabling a European civil pilot with a display authorisation to perform in the UK, but Trevor noted that "because we're now out of EASA, it's a lot more complicated and expensive."

Nightfire and balloons

Nightfire, with its pyrotechnic aircraft displays, ground-launched fireworks and the balloon night-glow all set to music, is a stand-out feature at the Midlands Air Festival. Trevor explained: "Balloon fiestas normally have a night-glow, which is blowing or firing the balloons to music. I created the Nightfire principle with pyrotechnic aircraft and turned it into a big night show with fireworks. It's quite an undertaking to get it all in sequence and everybody in the right place at the right time."

Balloons add greatly to the Midlands Air Festival's colour and family-friendliness beyond the evening show. Four mass ascents during the festival are planned, weather permitting, starting Friday evening and finishing Sunday morning.

In the UK, balloons can only fly early in the morning and in the evening when the weather and wind conditions are at their best and most stable with no thermal activity from the sun. Should the weather be unfavourable for free flight, organisers will try their best to put on a tethered or burner display.

More than 100 rainbow-coloured balloons will be involved this year, plus various special shapes including Thomas the Tank Engine, Snow White, Astro the Alien, Buster and Bella, Captain Jack, Oggy the Friendly Dragon and Up from the Pixar movie. The balloons and the rich mix of aeroplanes, helicopters, pyro effects and other attractions makes for a varied show. As Trevor said: "We've got to get people through the gate and keep attracting people with interesting things." ●

RIGHT • *Tiger Club Turbulent Team limbo flying in 2024.* MIDLANDS AIR FESTIVAL

BELOW • *Red Bull Flying Bulls' Bo 105C is another overseas rarity scheduled for 2025.* CORNELIUS BRAUN/RED BULL CONTENT POOL

AIRSHIP

Airship

A landmark anniversary for a widely recognised sight in the sky

ABOVE • *Goodyear blimp Wingfoot One over Oshkosh in 2015 – two blimps will be at the show in 2025.* DENNIS BIELA/ EXPERIMENTAL AIRCRAFT ASSOCIATION

BELOW • *Goodyear's Wingfoot blimps are 246ft long.* DENNIS BIELA/ EXPERIMENTAL AIRCRAFT ASSOCIATION

This year marks the 100th birthday of the Goodyear Blimp. To commemorate this landmark, two of the tyre company's airships will attend the world's largest airshow, AirVenture Oskhosh, in July 2025, the first time a pair of the famous airships will attend the event in the same year.

Blimp beginnings

In a January 2025 announcement, Goodyear said: "The Goodyear Blimp has been woven into the fabric of America for a century through countless cultural moments and historic events. Through the years, the blimp has appeared at marquee events, from the Olympics to the first Super Bowl, been featured in famous songs, movies and television shows, generated millions of dollars for charities and communities, and even aided the US military effort during World War Two."

Founded in the city of Akron, Ohio back in 1898, Goodyear started out producing rubber products, including horseshoe pads, poker chips and carriage and bicycle tyres, before moving into car tyres. It later diversified into rubber fabrics and coatings for aircraft and lighter-than-air craft, building its first balloon in 1912 and flying them in national and international competitions a year later.

In 1916, the company purchased 720 acres of land southeast of Akron to serve as a flying field and manufacturing site. This included Fritch's Lake, which provided power for a mill and a reserve for factories several miles downstream. Goodyear renamed the site Wingfoot Lake in recognition of its corporate logo – the winged foot of the Roman god Mercury, the 'messenger of the gods' and patron of travel and commerce.

The US Navy contracted Goodyear to build B-type and C-type airships during World War One. Test-flying of these craft took place at Wingfoot Lake, which the US Navy took over and operated as a US Naval Airship Training Station from 1917 to 1921.

A century of airships

Goodyear realised the large envelope size of blimps would make for an ideal promotional platform for the company. The company's first airship was the helium-filled, non-rigid Pilgrim in June 1925. Since then, there have been more than 300 Goodyear blimps, going through several generations as technology evolved.

A Goodyear blimp (the *Defender*) carried a lighted sign – called the

Neon-O-Gram – as early as 1930. Airships with ever-larger envelopes were introduced during the 1930s; with the *Enterprise* debuting a 123,000ft³ design in 1934. Goodyear built airships for the US Navy during World War Two and introduced a new generation of blimps post-war. There was a first live TV broadcast from an airship in 1955 at the Rose Parade in Pasadena, California.

Envelope sizes grew again, with the *Mayflower* introducing 147,300ft³ in 1963, while the 1966 Skytacular electronic sign featured 1,540 lights and animations. The Super Skytacular sign was introduced with the initial GZ-20 airship in 1969.

Goodyear's airship fleet expanded to new bases in Texas, Florida and Europe, with bases at Capena, near Rome in Italy and the Cardington airship sheds in Bedfordshire in the UK. The blimps became widely recognised thanks to their use providing aerial TV pictures for major events such as the Super Bowl, Indianapolis 500, Daytona 500, US Open tennis, PGA golf, Formula One Grand Prix racing and Kentucky Derby. A European-based GZ-20 covered the 1974 FIFA World Cup opening ceremony in Frankfurt.

Two GZ-20s worked during the 1984 Los Angeles Olympics. In the aftermath of the 1989 San Francisco earthquake and 1992 Hurricane Andrew, the airships' electronic sign was used to display messages to people stranded below, including directions to supply stations.

The GZ-20s were upgraded from the mid-1990s with LED signage. The early 2000s saw Spirit-class airships arrive, equipped with a new sign technology, EagleVision, providing improved high-resolution LEDs for text, graphics and video. Separately, in the early 2000s, Goodyear contracted The Lightship Group to operate Goodyear-branded American Blimp Corporation A60 airships in Europe, Australia and Brazil.

A new semi-rigid airship, the New Technology, designed with Zeppelin, was announced in 2011. The first example, named *Wingfoot One*, arrived in 2014, followed by a second in 2016 and a third in 2018. These gradually replaced the GZ-20s, the last of which was retired in 2017.

Centenary celebration

Wingfoot One is based in Akron, *Wingfoot Two* in Fort Lauderdale, Florida, and *Wingfoot Three* in Los Angeles, California. A fourth Goodyear-branded Zeppelin NT (simply named *Europe Blimp*), was introduced to European skies in 2020 and is operated by the Zeppelin team from Friedrichshafen, Germany.

According to Goodyear, all four blimps will undertake "an ambitious year-long schedule, primed to show up at more events, over more cities [and] engaging with more fans than ever before." The quartet is scheduled to fly to 100+ cities during the year. Two *Wingfoot* blimps will attend the 72nd Experimental Aircraft Association fly-in convention at AirVenture Oshkosh on July 21-27 at Wittman Regional Airport in Oshkosh, Wisconsin.

Goodyear blimps often attend Oshkosh – the first time was in 1971, the most recent in 2021 – but never have there been two there together in a single year. The current plan is for the airships to fly during the week, in both the afternoon and night airshows. At least one is scheduled to be parked near the EAA Aviation Museum during the event.

Michael Dougherty, chief pilot at Goodyear Airship Operations, said: "Goodyear Blimps have been a symbol of aviation innovation and adventure for a century. We can't think of a better place than EAA AirVenture Oshkosh to celebrate our 100-year milestone with aviation enthusiasts from around the world."

Rick Larsen, EAA's vice president of communities and member programmes, who co-ordinates AirVenture features and attractions, said: "There is no aviation event more 'blimp-worthy' than EAA AirVenture Oshkosh and to have two of Goodyear's airships over the grounds will make this year unforgettable."

Goodyear CEO and president Mark Stewart described the Goodyear Blimp as "an enduring symbol of both nostalgia and innovation for fans around the world" with a "unique ability to instil a sense of wonder in those who experience it – whether from on the ground or in the air." ●

ABOVE • *The blimps will fly during afternoon and night airshows at Oshkosh.* DENNIS BIELA/EXPERIMENTAL AIRCRAFT ASSOCIATION

RIGHT • *Goodyear blimps have been an enduring sight in the skies, even in Europe, for a century, as here at the 1974 FIFA World Cup opening ceremony.* GOODYEAR TIRE & RUBBER COMPANY

Team Raven

Experienced pilots flying Van's RV-8 aircraft in an impressive formation aerobatic display

Time runs fast in the airshow world. "One minute we're starting a display team, and 11 years later we're renowned throughout Europe and the UK," observed Simon Shirley, leader of Team Raven. Since their 2014 debut, the team flying Van's RV-8 self-build aircraft, based at Swansea Airport, have displayed widely at events in the UK, France, Spain, Portugal and Ireland. Previous years have seen trips to Belgium, Denmark and the Netherlands. In 2025, they expand from a six-ship to seven aircraft.

Fighter-like

Team Raven's origins lie in a Yak-52 formation school at Swansea, where Simon, a former RAF Tornado F3 fighter pilot, met fellow airmen Barry Gwynnett, Gerald Willliams and Chris Heames. They had previously started a Yak-52 formation called Team Osprey and decided to form a new team using the Van's RV-8, with Simon Shirley taking the lead and the callsign 'Raven 1'.

The name Team Raven plays on the letters 'RV' in the designation of the pacy, two-seat, fully aerobatic RV-8, a popular self-build aircraft, with more than 1,600 examples flying worldwide. According to the team's website: "The RV-8's 180hp engine has an excellent power-to-weight ratio, which combined with an efficient airframe gives the aircraft the performance and fighter-like handling that make it perfect for formation flying." Simon added: "A tandem configuration is much better for formation flying because you're always on the longitudinal centre of the aeroplane. The visibility is amazing. It's got a crisp response, but it's not overly sensitive.

"If you've got someone in the back, the aircraft is a bit more pitchy, but in its overall handling it's a nice mix between response and viceless. It's not got any quirky characteristics that are going to put you in trouble – if you get close to the edge of the envelope, it recovers very quickly.

"It's what we call a 'square' aeroplane – so it's roughly 20ft wingspan and 20ft long. You sit right on the main spar, the centre of gravity in the middle of the aeroplane. And they're light [1,600lb gross weight] so even though they've only got 180hp, you get really good performance.

"We want to display the RV-8 for what it is – we don't want a sequence that tries to make it something it isn't. It's not got a massive roll rate, it's not an Extra. We're not going to go up there and do what we call 'kung-fu aerobatics' – flicks, spins, Lomcevaks – because the aeroplane isn't very good at it. We cruise at 150-160kts and it's very economical, not just for display flying, but for the utility of taking an aeroplane somewhere with your bags and someone with you if you want."

Experience

Team Raven's display pilots have stellar credentials. As noted earlier, Simon previously flew the Tornado F3 and is also a qualified flying instructor on the Hawk and a QFI on the Grob Tutor and Grob 120TP Prefect in University Air Squadron and Elementary Flying Training roles. He's now a full-time Reservist QFI and flight commander on the Universities of Wales Air Squadron, flying the Tutor.

Raven 3, Pete Wells, built one of the first RV-8s in the UK in 2002. Subsequently, he built a Silence Twister, the aircraft with distinctive Spitfire-like elliptical wings. He started displaying the Twister solo in 2008 and the act later evolved into the Twister Duo display team, which he led for ten years and took to airshows worldwide.

Raven 2, Patrick Willson, has recently joined Team Raven for 2025. Raven 4, Paul Farmer, is a former RAF Chinook pilot (including display pilot) who previously displayed a Yak-50.

Raven 5, Mark Southern, is an ex-RAF fast jet pilot who flew the Tornado GR1 and was a Jet Provost QFI. His previous display experience was on ex-military jets, having owned and displayed a Hunter GA11 with Team Viper.

Raven 6, Gerald Williams, was originally a professional rugby player in Wales, New Zealand and South Africa. Now a successful businessman in the Swansea area, his extensive display-flying experience spans many ex-military jets – including BAC Strikemasters and Hawker Hunters with Team Viper – and a Yak-52 team in South Africa.

Raven 7 is Russ Eatwell, who was a Royal Navy Sea King helicopter pilot before crossing-over to fast jets.

LEFT • *Team Raven says the RV-8's "performance and fighter-like handling make it perfect for formation flying".* NIGEL WATSON

RIGHT • *The team separates into different elements for four-ships, pairs and singleton manoeuvres that interchange.* VISITBLACKPOOL

BELOW • *Team leader Simon Shirley said "the visibility is amazing" from the RV-8 cockpit, as can be seen here in this photo of a display at Weston-Super-Mare in Somerset.* TEAM RAVEN

He flew the Sea Harrier F/A2 on operations over the Balkans before becoming an instructor. He also spent two seasons as the Sea Harrier display pilot. He flew for the Royal Navy Historic Flight (today, Navy Wings) and Spitfires for the Rolls-Royce Heritage Flight and what is today Spitfires.com.

Lead and lag

Team Raven presents a fast-paced 13.5-minute display. Simon emphasises how the team wants no 'dead time' in the routine: "We don't want the whole formation disappearing to re-form and come back two minutes later. Having something going on in front of the crowd at all times is very strong in our ethos."

This is apparent when watching a Team Raven routine. After starting as a seven-ship, they separate into different elements for formation, pairs and singleton manoeuvres. The different sections interchange — as one element turns off its smoke after completing a manoeuvre, another appears for the next figure — before the entire team re-forms for the finale.

How does Team Raven achieve this flow to the sequence? The answer lies in a fundamental of air combat flying: lead and lag pursuit, where an attacker positions their aircraft to increase or maintain range to a target without overshooting. Simon explained: "If you don't control the overtake you can fly through the other side and not join the aircraft in time. If four of us break and I go away on the crowd-left 45 and start a right-hand turn to come in on the 'B' axis [the display line extending out from crowd centre], the other three following me will never join in time using power alone. The analogy would be, if you're trying to catch your dog when it runs off, you don't run to the dog, you run ahead of it. That's how we keep it tight, we use that lead and lag.

"You've got to be aggressive, because you've got to join with the other aircraft in short order, which makes it easier to generate closure. Your relative overtake is huge, and it's recognising the cues of when to control that, when to bring the throttle back. You can

use 'G' to slow down as well – we load the aeroplane, so you'll see the guys pull in and tighten their turns. That actually scrubs off some speed. It's that controlled aggression that allows us to join quickly. It sounds obvious, but the trick to keep something in front of the crowd – don't go far away. To gain the energy for an aerobatic manoeuvre we use height, then we trade height for speed for the next manoeuvre.

"I used to go quite a long way away and run in for a while, then I figured out that if I stayed close and went a bit higher, I'd get more energy back. So we just go steep and high, then tip in. You tip the nose down and you get the speed back, but you don't go far away."

Simon noted that the different elements never go further away than about a mile-and-a-half from the display area during the show: "If you watch our display, we use the smoke to bring people's eyes to where they should be looking. The other aircraft are never far away – you can see all the aircraft for the whole display."

Making life easy

Controlling energy and position is part of the team leader's job in a formation aerobatic display. Simon explained: "We've got to be in the right place, at the right speed and the right height. I try not to move the throttle. The other guys are moving their throttles whether I move mine or not. If I'm accelerating or decelerating, then it's hard for them to stay with me. My job is to make their life easy."

A leader's consistent application of controls is important: "I try and make things predictable. I try to keep the roll rate the same all the time. It's something you have to experience to understand how difficult that is. If [the other pilots] know what they're getting they can put up with fast roll rates. It's when it's variable that it becomes difficult. If one day I rolled right quite slowly, then the next day I did it quickly, that's going to catch them out because their muscle memory is around their input."

Smooth flying from the leader is important, said Simon: "Smooth doesn't mean lame and lax, it just means the same every time. You can still be aggressive and smooth, you just need be predictable and consistent." The cadence of the leader's voice commands matters, too, in helping the other pilots to anticipate their control inputs.

Coordination with Gerald Williams, who leads the second section when the team separates, is also important. Simon explained: "We stay visual with one another. We make the same radio calls in the same place every time, so when he says a certain thing over the radio I know where he is in space even if he's behind me. So I can start my turn back and I can 'play' the turn so I arrive at the right time."

ABOVE • *On board with the team as they perform a manoeuvre they call the Twizzle.* TEAM RAVEN

LEFT • *Controlling energy and position is part of the team leader's job in a formation aerobatic display.* TEAM RAVEN

Really hard work

Turbulence poses a challenge in formation flying. Simon explained: "Turbulence sometimes counters your roll and sometimes assists; it makes the roll rate variable. It's not more difficult to fly a formation in turbulence, but sometimes I'll put the stick to the right, a bit of turbulence will come along and it'll stop my roll, but the other guys will still be rolling."

According to Simon, display flying is "really hard work", but its challenges go beyond the demands of precision aerobatic flying: "You see us for 13 minutes, but the effort that's gone into that is phenomenal, not least of which is getting there."

When Team Raven displays on the beach at Oeiras near Lisbon in Portugal, for example, it takes the team seven hours just to fly there from the UK: "The effort that we make to get aircraft to display venues is the thing people don't see. Last year we ended up with an aircraft stuck in Santander in northern Spain for three days without a starter motor.

"The piece of display flying people never see, but which we actually hold as the highest risk, is the transit flying between venues. I'm not joking – the most dangerous thing we'll do in display flying is getting to and from the venue, whether that's self-imposed pressure, external pressure, weather, fuel, serviceability or people falling out."

Reputation

Team Raven has performed many displays in France in recent years. The first was in Dinard, where the team traditionally went with their partners towards the end of the season. Simon explained: "It's a tiny airfield. They didn't have much of a budget but we said we'd do the show as we were going to be there anyway. We did it and the organisers loved us. They told us that 'the only other people who do what you do in France are the Patrouille de France'. The organisers [at Dinard] passed on our details to other organisers and we've just exploded in France. We're actually having to turn people down."

BELOW • *Flying with a French Air and Space Force Rafale during a visit to France.* TEAM RAVEN

This year, Team Raven is expecting to perform shows in France at La Ferté Alais/Cerny, Le Touquet, Halbert and Cambrai. There's also the prospect of returning to Spain and Portugal and several UK seaside shows, as well as RAF Cosford and one of the Duxford displays. Simon said: "Make no bones about it, it's not the pilots that are the important part of display flying: 50% is displaying the aeroplane and its attributes, 50% is displaying a skill. It's a really hard discipline, and if you don't have discipline in display flying it can go wrong. A reputation is hard to get, and just as difficult to maintain. I tell the team: 'You are always on display, whether you're in a flying suit or not'.

"Even the way we line up the aircraft and when we're transiting. If we land at an airfield for fuel on the way to a venue, we like to look and sound professional. It's the way you deal with people. We're always polite. It's all about that image.

"I'm chuffed where we are and the reputation we appear to have. We love the welcome we get and people are very free with their praise – it means a lot." ●

SEASIDE

Seaside

Coastal air displays are some of the most popular airshows

ABOVE • Viewed from around 4,000ft, the Red Arrows arrive in Blackpool in August 2024 ahead of the town's annual airshow on the seafront.
UK MINISTRY OF DEFENCE/CROWN COPYRIGHT 2024

Aeroplanes flying in the wide-open space along the coast is part of the summer in the British Isles, accompanied by sunshine, sandcastles, ice cream, fish-and-chips, seagulls' cries and the breeze across the shore. Airshows at coastal towns in the summertime in Britain date back more than a century. Some of the country's earliest large public air displays were held in the famous seaside resorts of Blackpool and Bournemouth.

Many towns have organised large air displays over the decades. Several current British seaside airshows started as small town shows or local RAF recruitment fairs, typically featuring the Battle of Britain Memorial Flight, an in-service jet or helicopter or the Red Arrows.

From the mid-1980s, local councils in various coastal towns around Britain chose to run larger, more comprehensive airshows. Ray Thilthorpe, the Red Arrows' team manager in 1979-82, was the flying display director at several venues for many years. Southend, Sunderland, Southport, Clacton, Eastbourne and Folkestone all started shows. The annual Battle of Britain anniversary airshow over St Aubin's Bay in Jersey evolved, in 1997, into a larger international air display, including historic aeroplanes rarely seen elsewhere in Britain.

Many other coastal towns in the UK have held airshows of some kind over the years. Bournemouth on the south coast. Dawlish, Minehead, Paignton, Sidmouth, Swanage and Weston-Super-Mare in the southwest. Margate and Herne Bay in the southeast. Blackpool and Whitehaven in the northwest. Cleethorpes, Great Yarmouth, Lowestoft, Scarborough and Withernsea on the east coast. Llandudno, Rhyl, and Swansea in Wales, Ayr in Scotland, and Bangor and Portrush in Northern Ireland. Not all these seaside airshows have taken place each year. Some events (Llandudno, Margate) have been relatively shortlived, while others (Great Yarmouth, Swanage) have been one-offs. Others, such as air displays for Armed Forces Day in Cleethorpes and Scarborough, have been inaugurated more recently.

Over the long term, there's no doubt seaside airshows have become intrinsic to the British aviation scene, especially given a dwindling number of traditional airfield shows due to military cutbacks (base closures, changing operational circumstances, fewer resources), increasing organisational costs and tighter safety regulations.

Increasingly difficult

Seaside airshows themselves have encountered turbulence over the years. The challenge of funding free-to-attend events has proved too much for volunteer-run shows in Lowestoft, Dawlish and, most recently, Teignmouth in Devon.

In February 2025, Teignmouth's organisers said: "Despite the efforts of our volunteer committee, securing the necessary funds of £90,000 needed to host a safe and successful airshow has proven increasingly difficult. As a free-to-attend event, we rely heavily on sponsorships, donations and grants. Unfortunately, this year we are drastically short of the financial support required. In previous years our committee have fought tirelessly to raise the income needed, often only pulling it off in the eleventh hour – which is simply not sustainable."

Historically the seaside airshows organised by local councils were funded by town marketing/events budgets. But the squeeze on public finances – and, of course, numerous other spending demands on councils – meant these events had to cut their cloth accordingly. An airshow is expensive to put on, as the statement from Teignmouth's organisers indicated. In the face of spending cuts, several council-run events (Margate, Southend, Sunderland, and Weston-super-Mare) simply ended.

RIGHT • Airbourne at Eastbourne in West Sussex celebrated its 30th birthday in 2024.
ANDY SOLOMAN/UCG/UNIVERSAL IMAGES GROUP VIA GETTY IMAGES

Even the Bournemouth Air Festival in Dorset – which started in 2008, and, with an estimated half-a-million visitors a year, became Britain's largest airshow by crowd numbers – is not taking place in 2025. Organisers BCP Council announced before the 2024 show that it would no longer fund the event. The council is talking with a private operator about reviving a show in 2026. The organisers of the Pacific Airshow at Huntington Beach in California are interested, reported the *Bournemouth Echo* in late 2024.

RIGHT • *A Boeing Stearman wingwalking act from 46 Aviation Classics in Switzerland will perform at Eastbourne in 2025.*
REBEKA PÉNZES VIA 46 AVIATION CLASSICS

Revenue

Eastbourne Borough Council runs the four-day Airbourne show in West Sussex, which celebrated 30 years in 2024. The council noted in March 2025: "The cost of the flying displays and the temporary infrastructure requires financial support from businesses and airshow visitors to offset costs each year."

Seaside airshow organisers must be savvy in raising revenue and ensuring the continued viability of their events. Eastbourne Borough Council has worked on new commercial ventures for Airbourne including premium hospitality packages with seating and dining, sponsorship, car parking, merchandise and donations. According to the council, Airbourne was 'cost-neutral' in 2024 for the third year in a row.

However, achieving financial sustainability is an ongoing process. Councillor Margaret Bannister, Eastbourne Borough Council's lead member for Tourism, Leisure, Accessibility and Community Safety, noted in March 2025: "We still have much needed funds to raise to support the fantastic flying displays at the show, to ensure it is financially sustainable and to enable it to continue. We need your support to keep this show flying high – please do donate or show your support as a business with sponsorship if you can."

Torbay Council, which runs the English Riviera Airshow held in Paignton, Devon, said in March 2025: "Local sponsors, businesses and supporters as always have played an instrumental role in bringing the 2025 English Riviera Airshow to life. Their generous contributions, both financial and in-kind through essential event infrastructure, highlight the significant impact of the airshow on the local economy and community."

BELOW • *The Plane Sailing Air Displays Catalina G-PBYA over St Aubin's Bay in Jersey in 2024, with a backdrop of Elizabeth Castle.*
PAUL JOHNSON

Huge boost

The 'significant impact' Torbay Council talks about is exactly why local authorities in many coastal towns continue with their events. As well as Eastbourne and Torbay, events in Ayr, Blackpool, Clacton, Cleethorpes and Southport are returning in 2025.

Fundamentally, the essential thing about a seaside airshow – a family day out at the beach with some aeroplanes – remains very appealing to huge numbers of people. According to the British Air Displays Association, there were 2.8 million visitors to seaside airshows in 2024, which actually represents two-thirds of the total 4.2 million spectators who went to British airshows during the year.

Coastal towns recognise the footfall/revenue an airshow creates. Eastbourne Borough Council says Airbourne "provides a huge boost to the local, regional and national economy, bringing hundreds of thousands of visitors to the town [and] raising its profile". The English Riviera Airshow's marketing for 2025 urges people to 'Make a Weekend of it!', while Councillor Lynn Williams, Leader of Blackpool Council, said: "With the airshow taking place in the height of summer, we want to encourage visitors to make the most of this spectacular weekend – not just to enjoy the thrills of the two-day event but also to explore everything that the resort has to offer."

Ultimately, seaside airshows drive business to hotels, shops, restaurants, bars and cafes in the neighbourhood, and serve as a shop window for an area to encourage repeat visits at other times of the year. The midweek seafront airshows on Jersey and Guernsey are perennials of the Channel Islands' tourism calendar and an annual treat for residents (Jersey's children are given the day off school and markets close for the afternoon). Guernsey has moved its show to a Wednesday evening in 2025 to incorporate pyrotechnic displays.

Chicago to Murcia

Air displays over water are not just uniquely British, of course. In North America, there's the Milwaukee Air and Water Show in Wisconsin, the Chicago Air and Water Show in Illinois and the Canadian International Airshow in Toronto. (In the last two cases, with the flying taking place over Lake Michigan and Lake Ontario, strictly speaking these are 'lakeside' rather than 'seaside' airshows.) The 2025 Fort Lauderdale Airshow was due to have taken place in May by the time *Airshows of the World 2025* was on sale.

The Pacific Airshow at Huntington Beach in California is another seaside airshow in the United States. Pacific Airshow also runs Pacific Airshow Gold Coast in Australia. "We're the only airshow in the world with two editions!" the event says on its website.

European seaside airshows in 2025 include the Jesolo Air Show in Italy, the Malta International Airshow in St Paul's Bay, Valetta, and AIRE25 at La Manga del Mar Menor near Murcia in southern Spain. The last of these will commemorate the 40th anniversary of Patrulla Àguila, the Spanish Air and Space Force Aerobatic Team, and host the team's final CASA C101EB Aviojet displays before it moves to the Pilatus PC-21. The Red Arrows, Patrouille de France, Patrouille Suisse and Turkish Stars are also due to perform. ●

PYRO

The Ag Cat's pyros can be fired either manually or in a pre-programmed sequence. "It depends on the kind of shows we do," Jacob noted. Organisers often want the pyros set to certain pieces of music, which, Jacob explained, involves "a lot of the work to trim it in and synchronise with all the other things around. We have a basic show, but that can always be modified to what the organiser wants to do. It's getting the sequence right for the music – what kind of music we need to prepare for, or which switches should be pushed."

Flying challenges

Pyros released from aircraft must flame out before they reach the ground. In the UK there is a minimum pyrotechnic release height of 1,000ft under the Civil Aviation Authority's CAP403 Flying Displays and Special Events, the UK's air display regulations.

As utterly spectacular as they look to those on the ground, for the pilots flying aeroplanes and helicopters in fading evening light (or during the night in territories where it is allowed) it can be challenging to fly with intensely bright pyros and lights around them.

The Firebirds' Nigel Reid told *Aviation News* in 2023: "One of the greatest hazards is disorientation. On a summer's day, 30 minutes after sunset, it can still really be quite light, but cloud cover or a weather system coming through can make it pitch black. Keeping situational awareness is something we're very careful about. If the visual references are reduced, we'll do something much simpler to avoid the risk of disorientation. We're at 1,000ft anyway, but we'll take it higher if necessary or else cancel the display. The organisers are very supportive of that."

Several shows – such as Leszno – have ground lighting to assist pilots. The Scandinavian Airshow Ag Cat is also equipped with instrument flight rules navigation equipment. Jacob explained:

"For example, in Saudi Arabia, when you're flying towards the audience, it's easy, because you have the reference. But when you turn over the desert there's no horizon, so you're looking at the instruments. It's demanding flying. You need to know where to look."

How do pyros/lights affect formation aerobatics? Nigel said: "The number two [is] looking at an aircraft that's all lit up with the glow of the LEDs and fireworks. Both pilots being fully aware of which way up they are, and which way they're pointing, is really important."

Certain locations can bring added challenges. Conditions offshore at seaside venues, for instance, can present an undefined horizon, which gives little visual reference on height. Pilots must determine the position of crowds and display lines to ensure they do not breach air display regulations.

In the Firebirds display, Nigel Reid said: "Generally, pitching and rolling manoeuvres are flown towards the

BELOW • *Schweizer 300C Otto, once a stalwart in North America, is now based in the UK.*
PAUL JOHNSON

ABOVE • *Paragliders with pyro and lights during the 2024 Twilight Flight Fest at Oshkosh.* LAURIE GOOSSENS/EXPERIMENTAL AIRCRAFT ASSOCIATION INC

land, because it helps us keep visual references – you can see the beach line lit up. If we have a flat sea or low visibility conditions, we'll bump the height up."

Speaking about the effect of the high-intensity LEDs, Jacob Hollander said: "You want to use them in places [on the aircraft] where you're not blinded. You don't want the lights on the wings as the light would come into the cockpit – you want to have shadow."

Despite the challenges presented by pyro displays, Nigel said: "I've been lucky enough to do a mix of flying – military and civil stuff, big aeroplanes and little aeroplanes – but this really is a lot of fun. John, my number two, does a lot of Spitfire and Mustang flying, but he says what we do in the RV-4s is some of the best flying there is. Looping and barrel rolling with the fireworks running is really quite special."

Jacob Hollander agreed: "As performers, we're always looking to improve, to add or mix things and have a better display. We're looking into adding more lights and different pyro. I always think 'I'll make a show that I want to look at' – and if I want to go and look at it, I think it's OK." ●

RIGHT • *Airborne Pyrotechnics is a father-and-son team of two Grob G109 motor-gliders.* KATIE HUSTLER/MIDLANDS AIR FESTIVAL

F-16

An F-16 is always a highlight at an airshow – especially in an eyecatching colour scheme

ABOVE • *F-16AM E-006 popping flares during a photo sortie.*
ERIC COECKELBERGHS

There's no mistaking the Royal Danish Air Force Lockheed Martin F-16 Fighting Falcon solo display aircraft. Captain Troels 'Teo' Vang from Eskadrille 730 (Esk 730) at Skrydstrup Air Base in southern Jutland flies this unique example of the famous fighter, painted in patriotic Danish national colours.

Danish F-16s

Denmark was one of the four original European Participating Air Forces in the F-16 programme, alongside Belgium, the Netherlands and Norway. These countries jointly ordered 348 F-16s in 1975, all manufactured in Europe either by SABCA in Belgium or Fokker in the Netherlands.

Denmark's initial order comprised 58 aircraft (48 single-seat F-16As and ten twin-seat F-16Bs). The first of these arrived on January 18, 1980. A further 12 jets (eight F-16As/four F-16Bs) ordered in 1984 were delivered in 1988/1989, followed by seven more (six F-16As/one F-16B) in 1994-1997. Sixty-one Danish F-16s (48 F-16As/13 F-16Bs) were modernised from the early 2000s under the F-16 Mid-Life Upgrade programme, to F-16AM Block 20 and F-16BM Block 20 configurations. The upgrade introduced AN/APG-66(V)3 radar, colour multifunction displays, the LANTIRN targeting pod and AIM-120 AMRAAM missiles.

For many years, there were four Danish F-16 squadrons: Esk 723 and Esk 726 at Aalborg Air Base in northern Denmark and Esk 727 and Esk 730 at Skrydstrup, although Esk 723/Esk 726 were disbanded in 2001 and 2005 respectively. Danish F-16s have been involved in several NATO deployments: Operation Allied Force over Kosovo in 1999, Operation Enduring Freedom in Afghanistan in 2002/03 and NATO air policing in the Baltics and Iceland in the mid-2000s.

The Danish F-16 era is ending as the country switches to the stealthy, fifth-generation Lockheed Martin F-35 Lightning II. Denmark has ordered 27 F-35As. In March 2025, the Forsvaret (Danish Armed Forces) announced the F-35A would begin taking over quick reaction alert air defence duties in Denmark from the F-16 on April 1, 2025.

Changing times

Unlike other air forces to have displayed the F-16 at airshows over the years, the Royal Danish Air Force historically never had a single designated display pilot for the aircraft at any one time. Instead, up to three pilots from the squadrons operating the fighter would be trained to fly a set display sequence. The idea was that having several pilots authorised for the display was an efficient way to share the burden between operational units.

The Royal Danish Air Force transitioning to the F-35A had a knock-on effect on the F-16 display. F-35 customer nations base their first airframes in the US to establish an initial group of certified instructor pilots/ maintainers. These instructors then return to their home countries to set up the domestic training/frontline units. In the late 2010s, two of the Royal Danish Air Force F-16 pilots who were qualified to fly the airshow display were posted to the US to train on the F-35A.

By the time Denmark's first F-35As arrived in country in December 2023, the Skrydstrup F-16 squadrons had received another tasking: training Ukrainian pilots, technicians and groundcrew as part of the pledge by Belgium, Denmark, the Netherlands and Norway to gift Ukraine the secondhand F-16s they were retiring as their new F-35s arrived.

Teo, who has been an operational F-16 pilot for more than 20 years, was one of the other authorised display pilots at Skrydstrup. He explained what happened: "I said to the boss: 'Hey, this is going to be a challenging phase. I love the job. I don't mind doing it. I'm one of the last guys to transition to the F-35, so why don't you let me keep the display job – I don't need as much training as if you got in a new guy'. The boss thought that was a good idea, so I got to fly the display for a couple more years."

It is worth noting that in the Royal Danish Air Force, it has always been a tradition that pilots authorised for the F-16 display decide for themselves how many seasons they want to do the job. Typically, they do it for two to four years.

Teo observed that the Danish F-16 display pilots have always been highly experienced – the requirement is to be a flight lead with more than 1,200 hours on the type. For the F-16 display, he pointed out: "it needs to be a very experienced guy used to taking 'big-boy' decisions. If airshows want you to fly, but the conditions are not perfect, you need to be a grown-up and say 'Not today, guys'."

Using an experienced, trained and authorised pilot, and displaying at a relatively small number of shows each season (only around five or six events), works for the Danes: "We don't use many resources. It's a three-man job. It gives a lot of value public relations wise for a small amount of effort compared to a large display team."

RIGHT • *Captain Troels 'Teo' Vang is assigned to Eskadrille 730 (Esk 730) at Skrydstrup Air Base in southern Jutland.*
CAPTAIN TROELS VANG

BELOW • *The ventral fins beneath the rear fuselage have the insignias of the four Danish squadrons to have operated the F-16.*
SHAUN SCHOFIELD

Dannebrog

Back in 2019, Esk 727 F-16 E-191 became the Danes' latest designated display jet. It was decided to paint the fighter in a colour scheme marking the 800th anniversary of Dannebrog, the Danish national flag. Notwithstanding the COVID-19 pandemic, the distinctive red-and-white E-191 attended various European airshows over the next few years and was later selected as one of the F-16s Denmark would donate to Ukraine. The aircraft's last flight in the Dannebrog livery was on October 12, 2023, when it was ferried from Skrydstrup to the Royal Danish Air Force's maintenance facility at Aalborg for repainting into standard grey livery.

Subsequently, another F-16 (s/n E-006) was selected as the new display aircraft. This is a long-serving jet, having entered Royal Danish Air Force service in December 1988. During deployment to Afghanistan for Operation Enduring Freedom in 2002, it overshot the runway at Bagram Air Base. Following recovery by a US Army CH-47D, it was disassembled and flown back to Denmark by Royal Danish Air Force C-130. After repair and a rebuild, it returned to service

LEFT • *Captain Troels Vang said: "The view is amazing. You can look all the way behind you."*
CAPTAIN TROELS VANG

in 2006 with Esk 730. Teo said: "We decided the easiest thing would be to do the same paint [scheme] on a new jet, but it would also be boring'. The flag was great, but it was also very simple. And E-006 was probably going to be the last jet we were going to paint in Denmark – nobody's going to paint an F-35, especially not a small air force like Denmark – so we wanted to go all in."

The striking result unveiled on E-006 in 2024 is a second iteration of the Dannebrog design, based around the idea of the flag moving in the wind. Teo says: "People love the flag. We thought: 'Let's make it a dynamic flag'. The lines are actually shadows. When I fly, those lines coincide with the vortices when I pull G, which is cool.

"When we did the design, we had no idea if we would be allowed to paint a jet. We just did the design. I said I'd talk to the general and see how it goes. Lucky for us, he loved it and said 'Let's go'."

Teo asked the designer whether using metallic silver paint on the aircraft was possible to add to the effect of a 'dynamic' flag: "He's said 'Sure, design-wise we can do that. I've never seen it on a jet so I don't know how it's going to look, but let's go for it'. I think it looks awesome. It gives it a little bit extra."

As well as the flag on the top surfaces, E-006's livery marks 50 years since the F-16's first flight in 1974. There is a falcon design on the underside and the tailfin includes the falcon mural that Danish F-16 pilots wear in a patch on their flying suits. The two ventral fins beneath the rear fuselage have the insignias of the four Danish squadrons to have operated the F-16.

Display routine

As noted earlier, the Royal Danish Air Force had a set standard display routine flown by all of the pilots taking on the F-16 display duties. Teo said: "For many years we had a routine that showed off the best of the F-16, but we felt it needed an update. It was not ideal for the way people are reacting to shows these days. An F-16 is very fast, very agile and usually displays show qualities like 600kts, from one end [of the display line] to the other, and fast roll rates.

"We had a high-speed pass going straight into the vertical, where you climbed up to 27,000ft – you were trying to show the public how impressive it is for a fighter jet to go from 100ft to more than 5km altitude very fast, then spiral all the way back down. It is very impressive, but for the average person at an airshow what they see is a jet going really fast, really high and then it disappears – you can't see it. People are like: 'So, the show's over?' Nowadays, people's attention spans are short – it's the whole 'swipe right' or 'always scrolling' thing. Instead, we tried to make a routine that's closer to the crowd, with more rolling manoeuvres. An F-16 is an F-16, it's not an F-22. It can't do all kinds of crazy flips, but it is still very agile and very nimble. We try to have that as part of the routine."

After the take-off, Teo's full-height display features a half Cuban eight, a close pass, a reversal onto the display line 45° away from display datum (the centre of the display line the pilots use for positioning), then into a 360° maximum radius turn. Next, there's a half horizontal eight, a knife edge pass (this shows the Dannebrog scheme very effectively), then a contrasting 'high alpha' pass at slow speed. Alpha, expressed in degrees above the horizon, refers to the angle of attack or the difference between where the aircraft's nose is pointing and the aircraft's trajectory. After powering away from the slow pass, Teo positions the F-16 to face display datum for an 'on-crowd' loop towards the audience. Rolling off the top, he repositions for a slow roll before pulling into a double Immelmann. Exiting this manoeuvre, the F-16 is put into an inverted pass before a 'dirty' fly-by where the gear and flaps are extended. Next there's a high-speed fly-by and then a 'wave pass', a succession of barrel rolls along the display line, before landing.

Favourites

It's a pacy ten or so minutes and quite deliberately so. Teo explained: "Some air forces are more 'one manoeuvre, stop, new manoeuvre, stop'. Instead of having it split like that, we tried to make it more fluid. I love the barrel rolls. It's aggressive, but it's co-ordinated aggression with the jet.".

At the Royal International Air Tattoo at RAF Fairford, Teo noted: "The display line is enormous. It's a very long line. I start at one end and it's at least three rolls all the way along the line, whereas at other airshows it's one or two rolls and you're out of it. It's fun to make that happen, but you're almost on the minimum pull as you're going around. It's blending in different aspects of the controls to make nice even rolls."

Teo also likes the slow-speed high alpha flight: "It's such a difficult thing to set. There's a lot of finesse. There's no movement of the stick because it's in full aft on the angle of attack, then you control the power [of the Pratt & Whitney F100 engine] with your left hand to make it level. If you set it right and it's a nice day, it's fun – you're not really flying the jet, you're powering the jet along. Normally, we use the stick a lot for the movement of the aircraft, but we don't with the slow flight – you're just using the throttle to keep it level. It's delicate, and I like that."

Despite the flowing aerobatics, Teo does enjoy some of the more traditional aspects of F-16 display flying: "A crisp 360° max performance turn – once you set it, there's not that much thought going into it, other than just a lot of power, a lot of G and pulling. That also has a bit of charm, because it's so physical. You just go full throttle and max G. That's rewarding."

RIGHT • *The design on the top surfaces is based around the idea of a flag moving in the wind.*
NIGEL WATSON

BELOW • *Silver metallic paint on E-006 gives the aircraft "a little bit extra", said Vang.*
ERIC COECKELBERGHS

Teo's least favourite and most challenging manoeuvre is the slow roll: "It varies in length with the display line. Sometimes the slow roll has a different speed to others, because you need to start it and finish it on the display line before going into the double Immelmann. Sometimes you roll a little faster to make it fit the display line. It's tricky keeping the roll going at the same rate without losing altitude or pointing off the display line. It's co-ordinated with a blended stick, push and rudder on both sides of the roll, and also when you're inverted. It looks easy from the ground because you're just rolling the aircraft slowly, but when you're rolling slowly, there's a lot of push going on to keep up the nose in the middle of the roll. There's a lot of different control inputs going in. As a pilot, that's one of the trickiest manoeuvres – not to do it, but to do it nicely."

Pilot friendly

Teo loves flying the F-16: "It's a pilot's jet. It was originally designed by engineers, but it's been perfected by pilots. The way you sit in it is amazing – you sit a little bit back and you're on top of the jet. It's a single glass canopy, there's no canopy bow in the way of your vision, so the view is amazing. You can look all the way behind you, and almost all the way down as well, there are no canards.

"If you just had to fly it and not use any of the systems it's an easy jet to fly. Just point it where you want it and that's where it goes. The flight controls are easy. You sit with the stick to the side, not between your legs, so you have a good position. It's a pilot-friendly jet. It just flies great."

And for an airshow crowd, it displays equally as well. ●

GAZELLE SQUADRON

did stand me in good stead – not just the flying and the formation, but how to put the display together: when you break, how to rejoin quickly and neatly and what looks good in front of a crowd.

"The crowd likes to see four aircraft in different formations, so they can take photographs. They want to hear the noise and they like the fast, opposing passes with the pairs. It's quite easy to take those elements of what the Sharks and the Blue Eagles did – and which we know looked good – and put them into a display. It was surprising how quickly it came together."

Formation flying

A pilot in a formation of fixed-wing aircraft, whether it is a team of jets or piston-engine aircraft, uses specific reference points on a lead aircraft to align their machine with the formation leader. They follow the slightest movement of the lead aircraft, effectively making their aircraft an extension of the leader's. They use specific reference points on the lead aircraft to hold formation, making continuous, minor shifts in movement to stay in position.

Kev said it's exactly the same with a helicopter team: "If you are flying in line astern, you've got the anti-collision light on the tail on the top of the rotor head. For spacing, you've got to know what's too close – you don't want to get caught in the other guy's downwash ahead of you. If you're taking echelon left or echelon right, so you're behind the lead aircraft and you're on his left or right side, you're at the same height as him. For spacing you look to where the skids are on the aircraft, there's a cross-tube that comes down and holds the skid. You line up with the front bit of the [skid] on the other side [of the helicopter], so that gives you the diagonal, then you'll line that up with the one on the forward end on the other side to line those two up."

Helicopter formation flying must account for rotor blades: "Helicopter formation is always expressed in rotor spans, and the rotor span is the width of the rotor disc." A Gazelle's rotor span is 10m and the Squadron's helicopters are two rotor spans apart in formation, so each helicopter is 20m apart. The Gazelles are also parked 20m apart when they are on the ground. Before a display, Kev explained that "we all go out, sit in one of the aircraft and just look at the perspective of the other aircraft and just remind ourselves what 20m looks like."

Rotor spacing is judged visually in the air, so the Gazelle Squadron pilots' considerable experience comes into its own: "You know when you're getting too close – it feels uncomfortable. It's easy to judge the distance between the aircraft when you've done it a fair bit. It's also the job of number four to do the 'whipping-in' when we're running in for a display, so I'll say 'Two move out, three move in'. When you're at four, you're in the unique position where you can see the three helicopters ahead of you."

ABOVE • Ex-RAF Gazelle HT2 ZB627 (now G-CBSK) and former Royal Navy XX436 (now G-ZZLE). SHAUN SCHOFIELD

BELOW • Former Empire Test Pilots School Gazelle HT2 XZ939 (now G-CLGO) turns in for a pairs crossover. SHAUN SCHOFIELD

Turbulence

Kev said that wind doesn't really affect helicopter formation flying too much, but turbulence does, especially when positioning for the crowd during a display: "Over Teignmouth in 2024 it got quite bumpy and unpleasant – there are a fair few cliffs round there. The best wind you can have for a helicopter is 10kt off-crowd wind [a wind that's blowing away from the crowd]. It means that in my solo bit I'm hovering into wind, which helicopters like to do – they don't like further downwind or crosswind as it's uncomfortable."

Calculating the effects of turbulent conditions is especially important in the positioning of the crossover manoeuvres. Kev explained: "When we split into two pairs and we go to either end of the crowdline, there'll be a difference in how we conduct the manoeuvre depending on which way the wind is blowing. If it's blowing right to left, for instance [from the perspective of the crowd], the guys that are going downwind will pull up earlier than the guys upwind, because you'll end up in different places otherwise and you won't be crossing in the middle."

The Gazelle Squadron pilots have flown a lot of formation before, but

comprehensive pre-display preparation is mandatory under the UK Civil Aviation's air display regulations.

As well as a pre-display briefing, Kev explained that "you do what's called the 'dirt dive', where we will walk through the display two or three times. We'll do all the calls, we'll all walk round together, so everyone knows what they're doing. It's invaluable. We never did that back in the day [on the Sharks], but it's mandated now."

'Absolute joy'

Kev agrees with the often-used description of the Gazelle as the sports car of the helicopter world. The type's single 590hp Turbomeca Astazou IIIA engine delivers "a good amount of power" for display flying, but admits that it's "perhaps not so good round the hover, because the Fenestron [its enclosed tail rotor] was optimised for forward flying, cruise flight at 120kt".

In forward flight, Kev says the Gazelle "is an absolute joy to fly. It is very light and responsive on the controls. It's got a really good hydraulic system – it can be flown without hydraulics if they fail – and it's got a trim system so you can trim the cyclic. It's got fantastic visibility for formation flying. The instrument panel is not big, so you've got an amazing view of everything. The design of the rotor head is such that you really can throw the aircraft around – unlike a Jetranger, for instance, which has a fully teetering rotor head."

There are a couple of manoeuvres during the display that showcase the Gazelle's agility: "We do the standard wingover: you pull up 30° nose up, then as the speed gets to 40kt you roll to 60° angle of bank either way and as you fly round the corner you pitch the nose down."

A pedal turn is another feature in the routine: "You pitch 45° nose up and as the speed hits 25-30kt you put in full right pedal – you can only go to the right, you're not allowed to do it to the left – and the aircraft pivots under the rotor head and you end up pointing down. There's no angle of bank involved – that's all pedal."

Several limitations dictate the manoeuvres the Gazelle Squadron can perform in their display compared to those the Sharks and Eagles teams used to fly years ago:

"You've got the CAA Permit to Fly, you've got what the aircrew manual says – which is the definitive limitations of the aircraft itself – and you've got your display authorisation, which is issued by the CAA that tells you what you can do. When the Permit to Fly is issued for the aircraft, it has the limitations of the aircraft in there. In the Gazelle's case it came from the original military aircrew manual, which is the flight manual in civil terms. In there, it says: 'No aerobatic manoeuvres may be carried out'. The definition of an aerobatic manoeuvre isn't really defined anywhere, but for us it would be anything over 90° angle of bank and 45° angle of pitch up."

Other limitations stipulate that the Gazelle cannot be flown over a congested area on the ground, can't be flown at night, can't be flown in instrument flight conditions and can only take two passengers in the rear seats rather than the three it typically did in military service.

Step back in time

What manoeuvres does Kev especially enjoy? "At the end of the [solo] break-out, the guys fly towards me from crowd right in a vertical triangle and I go through the middle of them. It makes the hairs on the back of my neck stand up every time, because I hear the Fenestrons from all the aircraft whistle past."

Kev also enjoys the Roulette Break, "which was a Sharks thing. If you get it right on the day and you're lined up crowd centre, that's a great photo opportunity".

The Gazelle Squadron display certainly has many of those with the formation passes, crossovers and their eyecatching helicopters. It provides an unusual opportunity to see ex-military helicopters in formation, with the distinctive sound of the Gazelle's Astazou engine – which led to the type's affectionate nickname, the 'whistling chicken leg' – also part of the charm.

Kev said: "When you're displaying historic aircraft, you want to bring a smile to people's faces. Airshows aren't about derring-do with historic aircraft, it's just about people remembering 'Oh, I remember when I saw them, they were brilliant back in the day'. We're putting four aircraft in the air in close formation and allowing people to drift back in time." ●

BELOW • *The Gazelle Squadron recall bygone Army Air Corps and Royal Navy Gazelle teams, as here at the 2024 Wallop Wheels and Wings show at Middle Wallop.*
PAUL JOHNSON

FLYING BULLS

Flying Bulls

Red Bull sponsors numerous aircraft, from piston warbirds and jets to helicopters and aerobatics

The Flying Bulls team based at Salzburg Airport in Austria, which includes World War Two fighters and trainers, a classic propliner and helicopters, participates in various European airshows each year. Its origins are in Innsbruck back in the 1980s, when the late Siegfried 'Sigi' Angerer – a Tyrolean Airways pilot at the time – began collecting historic aircraft, starting with a North American T-28B, but soon expanding to include a Chance Vought F-4U-4 Corsair.

Angerer met businessman Dietrich Mateschitz, founder of the Austrian energy drinks company Red Bull, in October 1991. The pair's friendship evolved into a partnership and Red Bull's logo was added to the fleet. A loose network of enthusiastic pilots and technicians built up around the collection during the 1990s, but with space restrictions at Innsbruck, it was decided to relocate to a permanent residence.

Red Bull created the Flying Bulls as a standalone company in 1999 and started planning a new, purpose-built home for the aircraft at Salzburg Airport. The result was the one-of-a-kind Hangar-7, designed by Salzburg-based architect Volkmar Burgstaller. Construction began in January 2001 and it opened in August 2003.

Hangar-7 features a striking steel and glass dome composed of 1,200 tonnes of steel and 380 tonnes of glass. The building has 1,754 glass panes, no more than two of which are the same size. The hangar's superstructure covers 4,100m^2. Its main hall is around 100m long, 67m wide and 14.5m high. An adjoining building for maintenance and restoration, Hangar-8, opened in 2004.

American metal

A highlight of the Flying Bulls collection, P-38L Lightning N25Y (US Army Air Force serial number 44-53254) is the only example of the sleek twin-tail type flying in Europe. Preserved in a natural metal finish, the 1944-built aircraft served briefly with the US Army Air Force before passing into civilian ownership. Modified into an air racer in 1946 with a streamlined nose and clipped wings, the aircraft competed in air races in the US for decades. It was christened *White Lightnin'* in 1979 and competed regularly in the Unlimited Class of the National Championship Air Races at Reno, Nevada. Unfortunately, it sustained extensive damage in a landing accident at Greenwood-Leflore Airport in Massachusetts on June 25, 2001.

Red Bull acquired the wreckage in 2004. Following restoration by Ezell Aviation in Breckenridge, Texas, the P-38 flew again in June 2008 as N25Y. It was ferried to Florida and then transported by sea to Hamburg, Germany, where it was reassembled and flown to its new home at Hangar-7 in March 2009.

ABOVE • *The Flying Bulls often put up mixed formations of their aircraft, resulting in some unusual combinations of types, as here at AIRPOWER24 Zeltweg in Austria in 2024.*
PHILIP PLATZER/RED BULL CONTENT POOL

LEFT • *The Flying Bulls' P-38L and F-4U-4 Corsair performing at Sywell in the UK in 2024.*
JAMIE EWAN

94 AIRSHOWS OF THE WORLD 2025 WWW.KEY.AERO

North American B-25J Mitchell N6123J (USAAF s/n 44-86893), built in 1944, was an aerial firefighter in the US for many years, equipped with a belly water tank. It passed through various civilian owners and Red Bull bought it in 1997 and moved it to Austria in 2001.

Chance-Vought F-4U-4 Corsair OE-EAS was originally US Navy BuNo 96995 before going to the Fuerza Aérea Hondureña (Honduran Air Force) in 1960. It returned to the US under civilian ownership in 1979 and, repainted in US Navy markings, competed in the 1984/85 Reno Air Races. Red Bull acquired it in 1990.

Crown jewel

Flying Bulls describes Douglas DC-6B OE-LDM (ex-N996DM) as its "crown jewel". This 1958 aircraft was flown from new as the personal transport of the Yugoslavian president, Marshall Josip Broz Tito. The aircraft was used subsequently in the presidential/VIP transport role in Zambia from 1973, until it was abandoned at Lusaka Airport. In the 1990s it ended up in Namibia, where it was registered V5-NCF and received the name *Fish Eagle*. Red Bull later acquired the aircraft and it arrived in Austria in 2001.

Other pieces of American vintage metal in the Flying Bulls fleet include 1944 North American P-51D Mustang OE-LFB *Nooky Booky IV* (USAAF s/n 44-74427, formerly owned by Christophe Jacquard in France), and 1955 North American T-28B Trojan OE-EMM. Then there's the 1942 North American T-6 OE-ERB, 1943 Boeing PT-17 Stearman OE-AMM, 1943 Fairchild PT-19 N50428 and 1955 Beechcraft T-34 Mentor OE-ADM.

Cobra

The Flying Bulls fleet is not just fixed-wing aircraft. There's also a Bell 209/AH-1F Cobra attack helicopter, a type widely recognised thanks to its service in Vietnam. The Flying Bulls' example, N11FX, was built in 1967 as an AH-1F, then was converted to an AH-1S in 1976 and became a static training aid. The Cobra was fully restored for the Flying Bulls in 2009.

Aside from US machinery, Hangar-7 is also home to four former Luftwaffe (German Air Force) Dassault/Dornier Alpha Jets (OE-FDM, OE-FRB, OE-FAS, D-ICDM), a 1988 Pilatus PC-6 Turbo Porter (OE-EMD), and a 2000 Sukhoi Su-29 (N69KL). A brand-new Tecnam P.68TC Observer (OE-FSE) arrived in 2023. The fleet also includes the sole airworthy Bristol 171 Sycamore (originally XG545, now OE-XSY) and two MBB Bo 105C helicopters (D-HSDM, D-HTDM). The Bo 105C is renowned for its aerobatic performance, demonstrated in the Flying Bulls' displays with the type.

Mirko Flaim, the flight operations manager and chief pilot of Flying Bulls' helicopters, said: "It's fascinating what this helicopter can do, especially when you know how difficult a helicopter is to control."

A notable aspect of the Flying Bulls is that when multiple collection aircraft attend the same airshow, they often fly together, resulting in unusual sights, sounds and photo opportunities. At the Sywell Airshow in the UK in 2024, the P-38, B-25J, P-51D and Corsair flew in formation before performing individually.

RIGHT • *Douglas DC-6B OE-LDM, once the official presidential transport of Yugoslavia and Zambia.*
AVIATION PHOTOCREW/RED BULL CONTENT POOL

BELOW • *The Flying Bulls collection outside of the steel-and-glass Hangar-7 at Salzburg Airport in Austria.*
HELGE KIRCHBERGER PHOTOGRAPHY/RED BULL CONTENT POOL

Numerous other events have seen the Flying Bulls perform different mixed formations – such as P-38/Corsair, B-25/Corsair, B-25/P-38 and even a combination of B-25, P-38, P-51D, Corsair and two Alpha Jets.

The collection's 2025 calendar was a work-in-progress at the time of writing, but the Bo 105C is scheduled for the Midlands Air Festival in Warwickshire on May 30-June 1, marking their first visit to a United Kingdom airshow. On June 7-8, the Corsair, P-38, P-51D, B-25J and Cobra are due to appear at the Pardubice Airshow in Czechia. The Corsair, P-38, P-51D, T-6 and PT-17 will then go to the Oldtimer Fliegertreffen at Hahnweide in Germany on September 12-14 (this show is returning in 2025 after six years' absence), while the P-38, Corsair and a Bo 105C are scheduled for Festivolare Trento in Italy on September 20-21.

XA42s to Carbon Cub

Red Bull also sponsors the Flying Bulls Aerobatics Team, based at Josefov Airport in the small town of Jaroměř in northern Czechia, which flies four XtremeAir XA42 high-performance aerobatic aircraft.

The team's origins date back to 1961, when several pilots in the military flight-training school at Chrudim Air Base formed a team called Box

FLYING BULLS

Trener flying Zlin 526s. Box Trener stopped flying, but when Czechia became independent in 1992 after the Iron Curtain fell, its pilots decided to revive an aerobatic team.

Sky Box, flying the Zlin 50, was inaugurated in 1993 and began performing around Europe. They won the best team award at the 1998 FAI World Grand Prix of Aerobatics in Neuchatel, Switzerland. Red Bull sponsorship in 2000 led to a name-change to the Flying Bulls Aerobatics Team. It has subsequently performed extensively worldwide, visiting China, India, Japan, Jordan, Qatar and the United Arab Emirates. Various pilots have flown for the team over the years, but the current line-up comprises Stanislav Čejka (leader), Jan Tvrdík (right wing), Jan Rudzinskyj (left wing) and Martin Špaček (slot). Čejka, Tvrdík and Špaček are all Czech Air Force Saab JAS 39 Gripen fighter pilots, conducting Flying Bulls practices/displays in their spare time.

The Flying Bulls Aerobatics Team's display includes unusual manoeuvres rarely performed by other groups, such as perpendicular, climbing half-rolls and mirror formations. The team's website notes its style upholds the founding ethos of flying uncommon manoeuvres going back to Box Trener/Sky Box.

Italy's Dario Costa and Poland's Lukasz Czepiel are other European pilots flying for Red Bull. They respectively perform in an aerobatic monoplane, typically a Zivko Edge 540 or Extra EA300 and a CubCrafters Carbon Cub EX-2. The Edge/Extra are a familiar sight at airshows worldwide, the Carbon Cub less so, but this kit-plane's short take-offs and landings make for a striking spectacle.

Czepiela and Costa both previously competed in the Red Bull Air Race World Series, staged at various locations worldwide in 2003-2019, in which pilots flew aerobatic aircraft through pylons on a slalom course against the clock.

Miracle of flight

Red Bull aircraft and pilots frequently undertake novel publicity stunts. In 2018, the Matadors team of two XA41s flown by Paul Bonhomme and Steve Jones (both ex-RBAR competitors) flew in formation through an empty hangar at Llanbedr in North Wales – a true nod back to the barnstorming flying of the Roaring Twenties.

On March 14, 2023, Czepiela landed a Carbon Cub on the roof of the Burj Al Arab hotel in Dubai and took off again. The Flying Bulls XA42s looped in formation around a bridge in Podgorica, Montenegro, on October 24, 2024. Costa raced an Extra against a skier at low-level over the downhill course at Kitzbuhel in Austria in January 2025. These and other publicity flights (all fully authorised/planned) obviously occurred far away from airshows, but Red Bull aircraft/pilots do sometimes perform unusual and eyecatching feats at air displays too.

These often take place at the biennial Austrian Air Force Airpower event at Zeltweg AB. In 2022, Costa and Flaim flew an Edge/Bo 105C duet and, two years later, Czepiela and Costa put on a joint Carbon Cub/Extra display. The 2024 show also saw the Flying Bulls XA42s perform an unprecedented joint routine with the Czech Air Force solo display JAS 39 Gripen, where the XA42s barrel-rolled in formation around the fighter,. In a separate manoeuvre, one of the team flew in mirror directly above the Gripen, while the three other XA42s were stacked below the jet.

Red Bull's various activities at airshows – whether joint displays, aerobatics or the Hangar-7 collection – are all part of the company's promotional efforts across sports and entertainment. But the input to airshows isn't entirely about power, speed and noise. Red Bull also sponsors Team Blanix, which performs enchanting 'silent' aerobatics using two Let L-13 Blanik gliders. Based in Aigen-im-Enstall, Austria, Team Blanix describes its display as a counterpoint to other airshow acts. Their display includes mirror flight and multicoloured smoke. "Quiet, slow but no less dynamic" is how Team Blanix describes itself. "The gliders always leave an indelible impression on the viewer. It is not the power, nor the thunder, it is the simple miracle of flight itself." ●

ABOVE • *Mirko Flaim and Dario Costa flying an MBB Bo 105C and Zivko Edge 540 during a 2022 photoshoot.* JOERG MITTER/RED BULL CONTENT POOL

LEFT • *The Flying Bulls Aerobatics Team is based in northern Czechia.* DAN VOJTECH/RED BULL CONTENT POOL

BELOW • *Team Blanix: "quiet, slow but no less dynamic".* PREDRAG VUCKOVIC/RED BULL CONTENT POOL

THE DESTINATION FOR AVIATION ENTHUSIASTS

Key Publishing

Visit us today and discover all our latest releases

Order from our online shop...

shop.keypublishing.com/specials

Call +44 (0)1780 480404 *(Monday to Friday 9am - 5.30pm GMT)*

*Free 2nd class P&P on BFPO orders. Overseas charges apply.

Creating the Jet Pitts by integrating the turbines onto the airframe required detailed engineering design into every aspect of the aircraft. Analysing the impact of the engines on the Pitts' temperatures and weight/thrust characteristics was required. The gyroscopic effects from introducing turbines to an airframe designed for high-performance aerobatics needed to be worked out. Rich explained: "The main gyroscopic force on the aeroplane is still the propeller, but you've got two small jet turbines on the side. They are gyroscopes. All the gyroscopic loads add to the normal weight of the jet engines when you're doing aerobatics. All those forces have to be calculated. Analysing all those extra loads on the fuselage when you start pitching and rolling, and adding sudden stoppage with jet turbines, was quite a challenge."

As well as Eddie Saurenman, Rich worked with John Wighton, managing director of the engineering consulting firm Acroflight and former head of structures at Pilatus Aircraft in Switzerland, on the extensive analysis required to put the Jet Pitts through the regulatory process. Wighton designed a containment solution for the Jet Pitts' turbines to comply with European Union Aviation Safety Agency CS/FAR 23 regulations for the consequences on the airframe, fuel tanks and pilot compartment of a turbine rotor burst – put simply, an engine falling apart. Rich admitted that "at several stages in the process I thought 'It's never going to happen'", but the hard work over four years eventually paid off.

The Jet Pitts (appropriately registered G-JPIT) first flew in 2022. Test flying with the turbines was completed in January 2023 and presented no unexpected issues. Rich received full UK Civil Aviation Authority display authorisation for the Jet Pitts in April 2023. As Rich said: "In our own small way, with the support from our sponsors, we are aiming to inspire others into the STEM [science, technology, engineering, maths] world."

Rich is sponsored by Aerobytes, previously the main sponsor of Avro Vulcan XH558, along with The Blades Aerobatic Team and The Blades Air Race Team. Aerobytes is also the main sponsor of Aerobility and historically supported both the Shoreham and Dunsfold (Wings and Wheels) airshows.

Something different

What impact do the turbines have on flying the Pitts? Rich explained: "The aeroplane flies like an S2B. It's not so much having two little turbines, its really the turbulence they produce going onto the tailplane. There's a tremendous amount of drag – imagine flying an aeroplane around with two dustbins stuck on the side. Flying it normally without jets running, it's very draggy – until you put power on the turbines, you can't really do any sort of

ABOVE • *The Jet Pitts is a homebuilt aircraft, with wings custom designed by legendary US aircraft engineer Eddie Saurenman.*
RICH GOODWIN AIRSHOWS

propeller. The propeller produces a lot of torque and you don't have a lot of aileron control or airflow over the wings to stop it torque-rolling.

"You need to be very much more aware when you're flying the aeroplane that slowly hanging in the air like a balloon, you'll drift in a certain direction. It's no problem, it just takes more thought when you're doing your display routine. Even with a small amount of velocity over the wings – a small bit of alpha – you can keep control in roll a lot more. From an audience point of view, you can't really tell you're moving forward or up at 10-15mph, but that speed seems to be enough to control it in roll.

"People want to see it hovering at a reasonable altitude – you obviously have to stick to minimum altitudes for safety reasons. If there's catastrophic failure of engines, you need time to recover. It's not like you have an ejection seat. You've got to fly out of any manoeuvre."

Rich pointed out that one difference between flying the Jet Pitts compared to a standard Pitts is having to juggle three throttles for the Lycoming 540 and one for each of the turbines. (Incidentally, G-JPIT uses three types of Aeroshell oils: W100 for the Lycoming, turbine oil for the jets and Ondina for the display smoke.)

Spatial awareness

Which manoeuvres does Rich enjoy flying? "The knife edge flight – or sideslip flight as we call it – is always good. Transitioning from that is a great

BELOW • *Rich uses the turbine engines to hold the aeroplane in a hover like a mini-Harrier.*
RICH GOODWIN AIRSHOWS

airshow routine. You need at least 50% power to get back to where you are in a normal Pitts."

The two turbines each produce 700lb of thrust. With G-JPIT having an 8.5-litre, 300hp Lycoming O-540 piston engine, the aircraft has 1,700lb total thrust. The aeroplane weighs only 1,550lb, so it has a 1.1:1 thrust-to-weight ratio.

At various points in the Jet Pitts display, you can hear the jet turbines spool up as Rich uses the engines to hover the aeroplane like a mini-Harrier, before powering away. Seeing a little biplane fly in this way is "Something wacky, something different," he says: "It's unusual enough for people to want to watch it. The crowd want noise, smoke and something that's visually appealing."

The hovering generates a surprising level of noise, although Rich notes that it's fairly quiet in the Pitts cockpit: "Most of the noise is behind me, on top of the crowd. You've got full thrust on the jet engines and almost full thrust on the feeling. To go from take-off into sideslip flight, into going straight up, I do feel like I'm in a Typhoon."

Pilots clearly experience large G-forces in aerobatic flying, but Rich notes the Jet Pitts is actually slightly less physical than standard aerobatic aircraft. In those machines, he said, "you race along at 150kt and then pull a lot of G to go into the vertical to do something and then come back down and get more energy. [In the Jet Pitts, on the other hand] you can fly along at 100kt. You don't have to pull a lot of G to go into the vertical and you're going straight up."

Good fitness is still required for the physicality of airshow flying: "I'd love to say I get up and work out in the gym every day, but generally I try and run seven or eight miles twice a

ABOVE • *Rich Goodwin: "The crowd wants noise, smoke and something that's visually appealing."* PAUL JOHNSON

week – that's all I do to keep fit. I've been to body pump and Pilates in the past, but I don't work out like a Formula 1 driver.

"At the beginning of each season, when you start practising and training, your G-tolerance has gone down, so you have to build it up again. It's a mental co-ordination to tense your muscles at the right time to stop the blood rushing to your feet. The G I'm pulling is nothing like the unlimited monoplane guys, because they've got to have 150kt before they start doing stuff. To get into a vertical profile they have to pull a lot of G. We pull a fair bit of g in this thing, but we're rotating quite a lot. With this aeroplane, it's more the rotational and spatial awareness. That comes with practice. It's something you get used to."

Engine bearings

An eyecatching manoeuvre in the Jet Pitts display in its first couple of years on the circuit was Rich using the thrust from the jet engines to hold the aircraft in the hover, before performing a full 360° rotation from a stationary position. He explained: "I'll hold it in the vertical until we've got full right rudder against the thrust. When you do a normal stall turn, it's full left rudder, but with full right thrust helping you, it'll go right round. I've managed to go round two-and-a-half times.

ABOVE • *The two 700lb-thrust jet turbines create a lot of drag.*
RICH GOODWIN AIRSHOWS

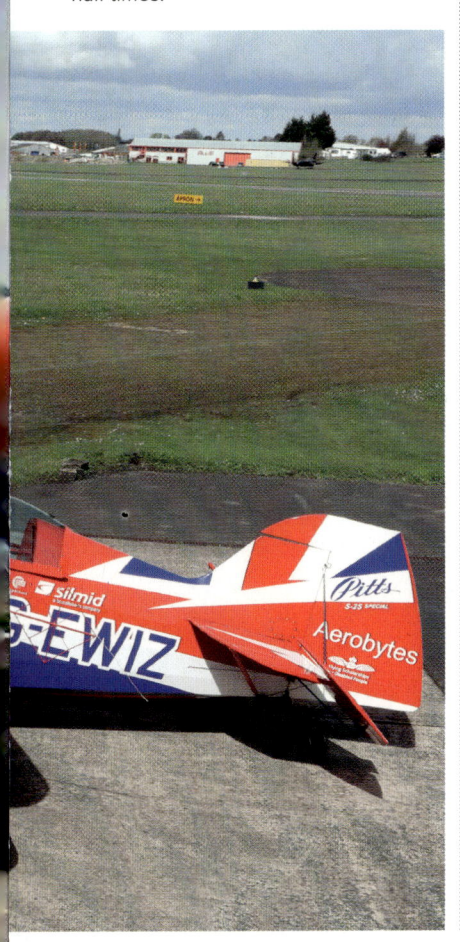

LEFT • *The Jet Pitts has a larger wing compared to a standard Pitts, as seen here with G-JPIT parked next to its stablemate, Muscle Biplane G-EWIZ.*
RICH GOODWIN AIRSHOWS

"One of the problems with this manoeuvre is that it's quite hard on the jet engines, because you're dragging those gyroscopes round in yaw very quickly. Any rapid yawing with an engine going at 4,600rpm produces a tremendous gyroscopic load on the bearings in the engines. We generally try to avoid that, because that's where the biggest wear on the bearings comes, when you're yawing the aeroplane against the rotors spinning round. I'm using the engines a bit more cautiously now." The bearings on the two turbojets last about a season and they need looking after to get them through. The team replace the bearings periodically as they learn more about the engines.

G-JPIT was in pre-season maintenance at the time of writing early in 2025. Rich explained the process: "We take the panels off and look for bits of the aeroplane that are failing. There are certain things you have to do – oil and tyres – and this year the propeller has gone off to MT Propeller [its manufacturer] because it gets a lot of grief from the sort of manoeuvres we do.

"A lot of people don't understand what goes on in the background. They see the flight for ten minutes and think that it looks like a lot of fun, but they don't see the level of time and commitment. There aren't many people on my team – there's me and another engineer, Colin Hales, and then it's calling in favours from people."

When the jet turbines had to return to the factory mid-season in 2024, for example, Rich rented a Cessna 172 midweek until he got the engines back and fitted to the aircraft for the next airshow.

Looking ahead

Rich admitted: "Like any innovation, it has had some teething problems. But in the two seasons we've done in 2023/2024, we've only missed a couple of airshows for maintenance. It's a pretty good track record. The display evolved from season one to season two, and I think we got it reasonably right in season two. I did a bit more on the B axis [the display line extending out from the display datum], but also more hovering.

"I'm going to try to produce some more high-alpha flying. I'm learning a lot more about how to hover the aeroplane and keep control of it in roll. I'll be trying to use that a bit more to my advantage. There'll be a couple more variations to the display routine, but it's the hovering manoeuvres and sliding at high alpha that I want to emphasise, because otherwise it's just a normal aerobatic display." ●

CLASSICS

There's Plane Sailing Air Displays' graceful PBY-5A Catalina *Miss Pick Up*, G-PBYA, Europe's only flying Catalina. The Fighter Collection has several American types including 1939 Curtiss P-36C Hawk 38-210/NX80FR (the last P-36 ever built), 1939 Curtiss 75A-1 Hawk 82/X881/G-CCVH (a veteran of the Battle of France and North Africa) and 1941 Curtiss P-40F Warhawk *Lee's Hope* 41-19841/G-CGZP. The company also owns Grumman FM-2 Wildcat JV579/G-RUMW, F-8F-2P Bearcat 121714/G-RUMM and Hawker Nimrod Mk I S1581/G-BWWK.

Bristol Blenheim L6739/G-BPIV and Westland Lysander V9312/G-CCOM are two relatively unsung wartime types at Duxford, both operated by ARCo. The Blenheim is the world's only flying example – it was a night-fighter with 23 Squadron during the Battle of Britain. Lysander V9312/G-CCOM is the only British-built example of this distinctive warbird in airworthy condition, and one of just a pair still flying in the UK.

Sywell Aerodrome in Northamptonshire is another notable base for historic aeroplanes in the UK. It is the home to a clutch of classics owned by Fighter Aviation Engineering Ltd. These include the sole airworthy Hawker Tempest II MV763/G-TEMT, Republic P-47D Thunderbolt *Nellie* 44-51942/G-THUN and Spitfire XIV MV293/G-SPIT in its Indian Air Force livery. Other aircraft in the Fighter Aviation Engineering fleet are North American P-51D Mustang *Jersey Jerk* A68-110/G-JERK, Lockheed 12A Electra G-AFTL and Hawker Fury FB.11 G-CBEL, its all-yellow underside representing the colours of one of Hawker's Fury prototypes. Sister company Air Leasing owns the world's only surviving Hispano HA-1112-M4L Buchon 40/2 G-AWHC.

Treasure trove

The Shuttleworth Collection at Old Warden in Bedfordshire is another jewel in Britain's historic aviation crown. Its vintage aeroplanes, motorcycles and cars recall the glory days of scarved aviators and motor-racers between the wars.

The Collection was started by Richard Ormonde Shuttleworth, who inherited Shuttleworth College and Old Warden Park in 1932 at the age of 23. A keen motor-racer and aviator, he amassed a collection of motorcycles, racing cars and aircraft during the 1930s. Shuttleworth was killed on August 2, 1940, when he crashed into a hill at Ewelme, Oxfordshire, while flying a Fairey Battle with the RAF Volunteer Reserve. After his death, his collection was put into trust by his mother.

LEFT • *Fighter Aviation Engineering's P-47D Thunderbolt is one of several classic fighters based at Sywell in Northamptonshire.*
JAMIE EWAN

RIGHT • *The Shuttleworth Collection owns de Havilland DH.88 Comet Grosvenor House, the winner of the MacRobertson Air Race.*
SHAUN SCHOFIELD

BELOW • *The Old Warden-based Bristol Boxkite was used in the film* Those Magnificent Men In Their Flying Machines, *which is 60 years old this year.*
SHAUN SCHOFIELD

Opened to the public after World War Two, it encompasses airworthy aircraft, agricultural and steam exhibits, veteran vehicles, classic motorcycles, bicycles, carriages and buses.

The collection has 41 aircraft according to the UK Civil Aviation's G-INFO database. De Havilland DH.88 Comet G-ACSS *Grosvenor House*, the aeroplane that won the 1934 MacRobertson Air Race by travelling from England to Australia in three days, is arguably the star exhibit. In its all-red livery, the rakish DH.88 still has a glamorous air about it even today. In 2025, it's 60 years since the Shuttleworth Collection acquired it. How appropriate such a fine aeroplane still resides in a collection started by a pilot who was part of the age in which it was built.

Other inter-war racers at Old Warden are the 1935 Miles Hawk Speed Six G-ADGP and 1936 Percival Mew Gull G-AEXF, the latter flown by the Spitfire test pilot Alex Henshaw from England to Cape Town in four days in February 1939.

The Shuttleworth Collection is far from just streamlined speedsters. As the collection's website notes, Old Warden is a genuine treasure trove of vintage aeroplanes from the first half of the 20th Century. There is Spitfire Mk Vc AR501/G-AWII, Hawker Sea Hurricane R7505/G-BKTH, Lysander IIIA Y1536/G-AZWT, Polikarpov Po-2 0094/G-BSSY and SE5A 654/2404 G-EBIA.

There are numerous types from long-gone British aircraft manufacturers. Among these are Avro Anson C.19 G-AHKX, Blackburn B.2 G-AEBJ, de Havilland DH.60 Moth G-EBLV,

CLASSICS

English Electric Wren G-EBNV, Gloster Gladiator L8032/G-AMRK, Hawker Cygnet G-CAMM, Hawker Hind G-AENP, Parnall Elf G-AAIN and Southern Martlet G-AAYX. There is also a 1909 Blériot Monoplane (G-AANG) and 1910 Deperdussin Monoplane (G-AANH), both restored by Shuttleworth before his death, and replicas of other types from the early years of powered flight in the Edwardian era.

Avro Triplane G-ARSG and Bristol Boxkite G-ASPP were built for the film *Those Magnificent Men in Their Flying Machines* (the Triplane was the mount for Sir Percy Ware-Armitage, played by Terry-Thomas). September 2025 marks 60 years since the film was released at the cinema.

Shuttleworth has made a couple of significant changes to its events calendar this year. Single-day air displays, traditionally held on Sundays, have switched to Saturdays. And there will be no dedicated sunset/evening events – these will take place instead during the Military Air Show (May 31), Festival of Flight (June 28), Summer Air Show (July 26) and the Best of British Air Show (August 30).

Dogfights and Turbulents

The assortment of historic types at British airshows also includes the only flying bomber aircraft from the World War One, the Historic Aircraft Collection's Airco DH9 E8894/G-CDLI.

There are various replicas of fighters from that conflict. Paul Ford has a replica all-red Fokker DrI Triplane (G-FOKK) and the Great War Display Team operates Royal Aircraft Factory SE5a and BE2c, Avro 504, Fokker DrI Triplanes, Junkers CL1 and a Nieuport 17. The team flies its aircraft in a choreographed re-enactment of a World War One dogfight, saying: "It is a unique chance to see up to six Great War aeroplanes flying together and certainly the only opportunity to see the aircraft performing as they would have in aerial battles with a series of head on passes and spiral dives and display smoke."

New to the scene in 2025 is Steve Jones' replica de Havilland DH.71 Tiger Moth Racer G-ECDX, which flew from Sywell on November 26, 2024. This is a full-size recreation of this monoplane, of which de Havilland built just two examples in 1927. Other classic de Havillands include Mark Miller's DH.89 Dragon Rapide G-AGJG and the sole DH.90 Dragonfly G-AEDU.

There are a number of display teams offering a nostalgic spectacle with colourful, easy-to-watch-and-follow biplanes: Tiger 9 with nine DH.82A Tiger Moths flown by members of the de Havilland Moth Club, and the Stampe Formation Display Team of four SV4B Stampes. The Turbulent Team from the Tiger Club at Headcorn in Kent also make a colourful contribution to airshows. They first performed in 1959, making them one of the world's longest-established display teams and they've flown at hundreds of airshows and events at home and abroad. Their energetic low-level routine with multicoloured aircraft balloon bursting, limbo flying and flour-bombing, still looks like nothing else.

Barnstormers

Team Mono, based at Sleap Airfield in Shropshire, is another display team flying light sport aircraft. Last year, the team consisted of Steen Skybolt G-IPII flown by Bruce Buglass and a tiny Taylorcraft Mono G-BMAO flown by Ben Gilmore. For 2025, the team has evolved into a four-ship: the Skybolt and Mono are joined by a second Mono and a Stampe, flown by brothers Tom and Ben Dews in a new act called the Barnstormers. The team says it aims to provide "a true homage to the flying circuses of the 1920s."

Lighter classic aeroplanes are inevitably best appreciated at smaller airshows, such as the Old Buckenham Airshow in Norfolk and the Little Gransden Air Display in Cambridgeshire. The 2025 calendar also includes smaller events like Wallop Wheels and Wings at the Army Flying Museum at Middle Wallop in Hampshire, and the Blackbushe Air Day; these may only have limited flying displays, but they do provide the opportunity to get up close to aircraft.

There are numerous fly-ins through the year, the highest-profile of which is the Light Aircraft Association Rally at Leicester Airport. An abundance of lighter classic aircraft can typically be seen at these events, including the Beechcraft D17 Staggerwing, Boeing Stearman, Focke-Wulf Fw44 Stieglitz, Messerschmitt Bf108 Taifun, Miles M14A Magister, North American T-6, Piper L4 Grasshopper and Pitts Special.

Broncos and Sea Kings

'Classic' does not necessarily always equate to 'ancient' – it might also mean aircraft and helicopters of more recent vintage, such as the North American Rockwell OV-10 Bronco, a multirole aircraft that was used for close air support, reconnaissance, medical evacuation, transport and even parachute dropping. The Bronco Demo Team, led by Tony de Bruyn, has become a popular sight on the UK and European airshow scene since 2010, having performed more than 100 displays at airshows throughout Europe and the Middle East.

BELOW • *Tony de Bruyn's North American Rockwell OV-10B Bronco, a distinctive sight at airshows.*
SHAUN SCHOFIELD

Ex-Luftwaffe OV-10B G-ONAA (wearing the code 99+18) is authorised to operate to the OV-10B's full original design flight envelope, including short take-off and landing operations and aerobatics. With its large wing, twin tails and the highly distinctive tone from its twin turboprop engines, the Bronco is a unique presence. De Bruyn's performance highlights its ability to manoeuvre in a relatively tight area.

Incidentally, there is another ex-Luftwaffe OV-10B on the European airshow circuit: F-AZKM owned by the Musée Européen de l'Aviation de Chasse (MEAC) at Montélimar in France. Last year, MEAC flew a Conair Turbo Firecat (F-AYKM) and has plans to operate both aircraft as a pair at airshows.

Another distinctive classic on the UK civil register is the Westland Sea King helicopter.

A British licence-built version of the Sikorsky S-61, the Sea King was used by the UK military in various roles, including anti-submarine warfare, transport and airborne early warning and control, as well as by Royal Marine commandos. However, it was search and rescue that made the Sea King such a widely-recognised aircraft with the British public, thanks to its deployment with the Royal Navy (red and grey livery) and the RAF (yellow livery).

ABOVE • *Historic Helicopters' Westland Sea King HAR3 XZ597/G-SKNG.* SHAUN SCHOFIELD

BELOW • *The Turbulent Team and, in the background, the Tiger 9 team of de Havilland Tiger Moths.* MIDLANDS AIR FESTIVAL

Historic Helicopters, based in Chard, Somerset, owns Sea King HAR3 XZ597/G-SKNG, painted in the all-yellow livery it wore during its days with the RAF. Retired by the UK Ministry of Defence in 2016, it returned to flight in civil ownership in 2020. There's no mistaking it at airshows, whether it's on static display or undertaking a search and rescue demo to highlight its past life. The helicopter also made an appearance in the 2021 BBC1 thriller series *Vigil*.

Historic Helicopters owns another ex-RAF Sea King HAR3 (XZ588/G-SEAK) and many other Westland helicopters: ex-Royal Navy Sea King HC4 ZA314/G-CMDO and HC4 ZF122, two former Belgian Air Force Sea King Mk48s (RS02 and RS04), ex-Royal Navy Sea King HAS5 XV647, former Army Air Corps Westland Lynx AH7 XZ616/G-LYKX, Wessex HU5 XT761/G-WSEX, Wessex HU5 XT771, Westland Whirlwind HAR10 XJ729 and a Westland Widgeon.

These are not the only ex-military helicopters in civil hands in the UK. There's another former Army Air Corps Lynx AH7 (XZ179/G-NCKS) and the various Westland/Aérospatiale Gazelles associated with the Gazelle Squadron (see page 90). ●

RIAT

Organising the aircraft participation at the Royal International Air Tattoo at RAF Fairford

The Royal International Air Tattoo (RIAT) at RAF Fairford in Gloucestershire is a three-day event with a huge static park, 18 hours of flying displays and an extensive range of ground attractions, including the interactive Techno Zone and RAF Experience. Changing times mean that the long rows of fighter, tanker and transport aircraft typically seen at the event in the 1980s and 1990s are now largely now a thing of the past. With 200+ aircraft from up to 30 nations and almost 170,000 public visitors, RIAT remains the world's largest military airshow.

RIAT is organised by the RAF Charitable Trust Enterprises (RAFCTE), which has a permanent staff based at Fairford. Running such a huge event is an immense challenge, from planning site infrastructure, hospitality/catering and ground events, to organising traffic management, crew accommodation/transport and corporate/VIP activities among myriad tasks. And that's all before you consider anything to do with aircraft, airside operations, fuel or air traffic control.

During show week, from the first aircraft arriving on the Wednesday to the last departure the following Monday, a 3,500-strong volunteer force helps to run the show.

The process

So what's involved in putting together the extensive aircraft participation seen at Fairford every summer?

Peter Reoch, RIAT's Head of Air Operations, described it as "a stable process, a well-trodden path" that begins the previous spring. As Peter explained: "The work in earnest for the next show starts at the event prior, having conversations with people seeing where you can build and improve. We do a strategic look-ahead, so we have an idea of what the theme for the following year will be."

Eyes in the Skies was set as the operational theme for the 2025 show. July to September are the key months for invitations/applications for the following year: "We write formal invitation letters to the world's military air forces and send them via their defence attachés in their embassies in London. They detail the plans for the event and the specific aircraft we'd like to see at next year's show, explaining their relevance to the theme. For some nations, we'll invite flying and static aircraft, some we'll just invite static [items] that might be relevant. For others that don't have that particular role of aircraft, it'll be a generic invitation for them to join us.

"When we do those invitation letters, we go through each nation's inventory, looking at what's new, what's about to retire and any changes." The advancing age of aircraft like the Panavia Tornado or Soviet-era MiGs and Sukhoi aircraft are "high priority" for the Air Operations team, he said.

Peter notes the application process differs slightly depending on the

BELOW • *This year's Eyes in the Skies theme highlights the vital role of aerial surveillance, airborne early warning, maritime patrol and search.* SHAUN SCHOFIELD

ABOVE • *RIAT in Gloucestershire is the world's largest military airshow.* ROYAL INTERNATIONAL AIR TATTOO

RIGHT • *The Finnish Air Force will display the F/A-18C Hornet at RIAT in 2025.* SHAUN SCHOFIELD

country: "Some European nations also have application forms to fill in; likewise, the UK military. With civilian aircraft, there are types we want to try and attract for a theme, whether they're privately owned or commercially operated, and we have an application process for civilian organisations that want to bring their aircraft. We're very lucky at RIAT in that that's quite a long list."

Allocations

Applications to overseas nations are submitted in the autumn. It's then a waiting game to find out what invites have been accepted – it's not the case that RIAT 'books' military aircraft, as some might assume. The event applies for support to an air arm, which then allocates the aircraft if it wants to support the event.

RIAT starts to hear back from invited nations about whether they will attend and what they will send during the spring. It's at this point when the administrative task for the Air Operations team really steps up: "Generally, there'll be informal conversations, meetings and phone calls to say 'We're thinking of sending this aircraft, but do you have a certain bit of equipment?' [or] 'If we send this aircraft, what day would it need to arrive and leave?'."

Planning can be straightforward in some cases – "We know them, and they know us" – but other items, including rarely-seen aircraft, "generally need a higher level of engagement and negotiation."

If an air arm unveils a special colour scheme on an aircraft, to mark an anniversary for example, the team takes note: "Sometimes we'll re-engage with the air force and say 'We'd be really interested if this particular jet comes to the show'. It's worth pointing out that when we're expecting a pair of aircraft, the policy is to try to get a special scheme but also a standard-painted aircraft. When the Italian Air Force sent U-208s to the show in 2023, we asked them to bring one in a special paint scheme and one in standard markings, so enthusiasts get the best of both worlds."

Co-ordinating aircraft participation is about far more than just the aircraft themselves. It's all the things most people don't see when they visit an airshow – having the right support equipment/fuel and handling

RIAT

ABOVE • RIAT will sometimes engage with an air force for specific airframes, including those with special colour schemes, such as this Italian Air Force Tornado.
SHAUN SCHOFIELD

1,500+ air and ground crew, including where they'll be accommodated and how they'll be transported around.

Reputation

Military air arms in the West are smaller than they were decades ago, with less resources to spare on airshow participation. Does this make it more challenging for RIAT to get support these days? Peter said: "It's a complex question. I would say we're really lucky at RIAT with our reputation. Global air arms and the attachés in London know RIAT. The unique selling point for us is that we invite the chiefs – the RAF hosts the Global Air and Space Chiefs Conference [at RAF Fairford] in the week before the show. When a chief goes to the show, they know what they're getting – or, if they haven't been, their predecessor will have told them. We've seen in the past that a nation's chief might come to the show, have a great time and they're more likely to send an aircraft. We're lucky in that we get that level of support, circa 25 to 30 nations every year, which is a lot higher than anyone else in Europe."

RIAT's 50 years of history helps too, Peter acknowledged: "We appreciate that we're in a unique position thanks to the legacy of the event. The challenge sometimes is getting those new air arms, or nations that haven't been for a while, versus a European operator who comes back year-on-year."

A comprehensive showing by US military aircraft has long been a feature at RIAT. Peter explained how their participation comes about: "The process has always been that the US embassy in each country is responsible for compiling a list of airshows/events they deem worthy of support. For us, the US Embassy in London will send out a message to all the airshows in the UK. We have to fill out an application form, which goes to US Air Forces-Europe and Africa [USAFE-AFA], but also the standard US Department of Defense DD2535 application form. We then submit those forms.

"In Europe, USAFE is the tasking and approval authority for all US DoD assets coming to an airshow. Once we're approved, they'll look at what assets are available. The change in recent years is that there's now a policy in place that aircraft stationed in the continental US are not permitted to come to Europe solely for the purpose of public outreach, which obviously is how airshows are categorised. They have to already be in Europe on an operational mission to be able to attend. That's the same for all European airshows."

All shapes and sizes

The Air Operations team at Fairford has a wish list of participants: "The wish-list changes annually, based on the theme. It's about making a balanced event so it's not just fast jets or just transports or just helicopters. I think what makes RIAT special is that you get to see all shapes and sizes of aircraft.

"We look at balancing – we don't necessarily want to have all F-16s in the flying programme one year, then none the following year. It would be better to have two F-16s in 'Year A', then a different two F-16s in 'Year B'. When we do the invitations, we think about the display assets that are available and try and alternate where possible."

Practicality does come into it, Peter admitted: "Sometimes, anniversaries drive it, whereas for other years we're looking for a rotation of different themes so we're not having three or four years of themes that are very fighter-focused, then two or three years of a transport or helicopter focus. It's about alternating them. For 2025 we are more focused on rotary and large aircraft, whereas last year with the F-16 and test flying themes there were more fast jets."

ABOVE • *The Friends of the Royal International Air Tattoo enclosure at RIAT 2024.* ROYAL INTERNATIONAL AIR TATTOO

BELOW • *A view over RAF Fairford during RIAT 2024.* TECH SGT JESSICA AVALLONE/ US AIR FORCE

Eyes in the Skies

The 2025 operational theme, Eyes in the Skies, is all about aerial surveillance, airborne early warning, maritime patrol, search and rescue, reconnaissance and signals intelligence: "The wish-list involves having different representations of, for example, AWACS [airborne warning and control system] aircraft – so an E-3, an Embraer E-99, a Wedgetail, etc – so we can show different models. A line up of different AWACS aircraft from different manufacturers is high on my wish list. For each nation we've got specific targets for the theme. ISTAR [intelligence, surveillance, target acquisition, reconnaissance] assets are some of the most highly tasked assets, and they are generally smaller fleets. We have to have pragmatism and see what turns out."

RIAT is also incorporating relevant civilian aircraft: "We've booked the Catalina for static display, and the aspiration is to park that alongside modern maritime patrol aircraft. We've got a Lockheed Electra coming from Sywell and the aspiration is to park that alongside aircraft used for aerial reconnaissance, to show the evolution of aerial photography from when it was first developed in the 1930s and 1940s to the capabilities air forces have today. I would also like to see participation of unmanned aircraft systems as part of the theme, so I hope we will have examples of remotely piloted air systems flying into Fairford for the show."

Making memories

Peter said it is paramount to have unique moments in the RIAT flying display: "We have wish-lists of individual display items we'd like to see, but also what we can do to make each year's show a little bit special."

The USAF Lockheed U-2S in 2024 – the famous spyplane's first appearance in a UK flying display for more than 30 years – was such a moment. There were also special flypasts in 2024 marking NATO's 75th anniversary and the BAE Systems Hawk jet trainer's 50th birthday. Peter noted: "A lot of flypasts are driven by anniversaries and special events – because of the approvals process and the associated work and time that goes into planning those, there needs to be a reason to do something."

But making RIAT memorable is not just about the flying: "I think the best airfield arrangement you can have – particularly for the non-enthusiast – is the ability to see a certain type of aircraft in the air, then be able to look at it on the ground, chat to the crew and, in some cases, get on board the aircraft.

"The RAF Charitable Trust's mission is to inspire young people into a career in aviation or STEM [science, technology, engineering, maths]. That to me is what sets RIAT – and other land-based airshows – apart. You can have that physical connection to the aircraft: 'I really enjoyed that display, let's find that aircraft on the ground

RIAT

and talk to the crew, buy a patch, sit in the cockpit'. That element of the static display is really important."

Peter added that RIAT has tried in recent years to emphasise aircrew engagement: "Making sure the crew that bring an aircraft are talking to the public, selling their squadron merchandise and facilitating access where possible.

"We're bringing in more sets of airstairs than we ever had before, so more people can get on board the larger aircraft and interact with aviation in a way they can't elsewhere."

Fairford's 40th

With RIAT's static display containing dozens more aircraft than the next-largest military airshows, the parking plan is highly complex. Any creative intent – for example, in 2024, all the F-16s were arranged in a line in chronological order of block for the type's 50th birthday – must meet operational constraints.

Peter explained: "We have an aspiration to make the static display layout as creative and relevant as possible. What happens in June, as we get closer to the show and we look at all the arrival times of the aircraft, is that it has to be balanced with the reality. For example, if a certain aircraft isn't arriving until Thursday afternoon or Friday, but other aircraft want to arrive earlier on the Wednesday morning. Where it's suitable to park them, any ground handling characteristics, towing and handling them, all form part of the considerations to create the aircraft parking plan to try and make the best of both worlds – to give the visitor the best experience as they walk round, but also be achievable given the constraints."

The 2025 static park may include a section highlighting 40 years of the event at Fairford: "We looked at what was here in 1985, and then which types are still in service, reviewing airframes that are still airworthy."

Several types in service four decades ago are still around today, such as Luftwaffe Panavia Tornado, NATO Boeing E-3A and USAF Boeing KC-135. There are even specific airframes present at Fairford in 1985 that remain in use, including Red Arrows Hawk T1 XX322, RAF Chinook ZA710, two Royal Danish Air Force F-16s (E-611 and ET-615) and USAF KC-135 59-1511 (a KC-135A at the time, now assigned to the 100th Air Refueling Wing at RAF Mildenhall). Several other 1985 participants, including ex-Royal Aircraft Establishment Gazelle ZB627 (now G-CBSK), fly on the civil register.

Peter said: "We're looking at the art of the possible. But before we commit to it, my preference is making sure we can do it justice. My aspiration is to have a number of aircraft, park them together with signage, but there's so much history over those 40 years that we need to make sure we don't bite off more than we can chew."

ABOVE • *A UK debut in 2025 is a Portuguese Air Force AW101 Merlin performing a search and rescue demo to illustrate the Eyes in the Skies theme.* PETER REOCH

BELOW • *These days, US military aircraft stationed in the continental US must already be in Europe on an operational mission to appear at an airshow.* SHAUN SCHOFIELD

Looking ahead

Peter said: "We're already thinking about the 2026, 2027 and 2028 shows now. We strategically look at themes – some up to ten years ahead – when we know there are key anniversaries, thinking about what we'd like to do and any building blocks we need to introduce over the coming years to achieve our ambitions."

Sometimes "the stars align, and we know a lot further out", Peter said. "For example, 2029 will be 20 years since the first flight of the Airbus A400M and 75 years since the first flight of the C-130 Hercules. To me that means we'll be doing an airlift theme for 2029."

More broadly, Peter said: "I hope airshows are still viewed as important public engagement pieces by air arms. As time has progressed, the variety of aircraft in certain fleets has diminished, but types in other areas is increasing. One example is training fleets. Across Europe there's an assortment of aircraft being introduced, for example the Polish Air Force using the Korean F/A-50. On the transport aircraft front, for many years the C-130 was the machine of choice for everyone. Now a number of those operators are replacing it with the Embraer KC-390 and Leonardo C-27. There's still plenty of unique types and there'll still be variety. It's making sure we make the most of that to ensure RIAT always delivers an exciting, eclectic mix of aviation.

"Airshows still have a massive role to play in public engagement, so people can see what air forces are doing, but also in inspiring the future. We know there's career shortages in STEM, aerospace engineers and pilots. Having an opportunity to get close to military aviation is more important than ever before." ●